POLITICAL DISCOURSE AND NATIONAL IDENTITY IN SCOTLAND

For our daughters: Elena, Bronwyn and Emma

POLITICAL DISCOURSE AND NATIONAL IDENTITY IN SCOTLAND

Murray Stewart Leith and Daniel P. J. Soule

EDINBURGH
University Press

© Murray Stewart Leith and Daniel P. J. Soule, 2011, 2012

First published in 2011 by
Edinburgh University Press Ltd
22 George Square, Edinburgh EH8 9LF
www.euppublishing.com

This paperback edition 2012

Typeset in Goudy Old Style by
Iolaire Typesetting, Newtonmore, and
printed and bound in Great Britain by
CPI Group (UK) Ltd, Croydon CR0 4YY

A CIP record for this book is available from the British Library

ISBN 978 0 7486 3736 2 (hardback)
ISBN 978 0 7486 6858 8 (paperback)

The right of Murray Stewart Leith and Daniel P. J. Soule
to be identified as authors of this work has been asserted in
accordance with the Copyright, Designs and Patents Act 1988.

Contents

Tables and Figures

Acknowledgements

There are many individuals that we would both like to thank for their aid, advice and comments along the way. We would especially like to thank those colleagues who have supported us during the research and writing of this book. While many individuals have read this and earlier versions of the work, and freely offered their criticisms and comments, we would especially like to thank Sarah Oates, Sarah Armstrong and Martin Steven, from the University of Glasgow, Duncan Sim at the University of the West of Scotland, Andrew Mycock at the University of Huddersfield, Christine Bengston in New Zealand, Sheila Croucher in Ohio and David Carwell in Illinois. Various drafts of these chapters have been presented at numerous conferences and our thanks go to our peers for their feedback from those events. Bonnie Steves also deserves thanks for freeing up time for this book to be written.

We would like to acknowledge the professional contributions of data from the British and Scottish Social Attitudes Surveys, as well as from numerous General Election and Scottish Parliamentary Election Studies. For accessing such data we thank the UK Data Archive, the Economic and Social Research Council and the original investigators and researchers involved in all those studies. The numerous scholars of the Comparative Manifesto Project, for their extensive and award-winning work on the field of election programme analysis, deserve credit beyond measure. During the fieldwork phase of this research many individuals took time out of their busy political and parliamentary schedules to engage in discussion and debate. Their insights and comments have greatly aided our work, and, although we promised to name no names, we would like to thank them for both their time and thoughts.

And finally, to our families, the people who have supported us all along, supplying enthusiasm and sustaining us, our thanks to you most of all.

Preface

Should you find yourself walking down Edinburgh's Canongate, you will find there, inscribed on the wall of the Scottish Parliament building, these words of Sir Alexander Gray:

> This is my country
> the land that begat me
> these windy spaces
> are surely my own
> and those who here toil
> in the seat of their faces
> are flesh of my flesh
> and bone of my bone.

Here, as you stand looking at the modernist architectural dream that is the home of Scotland's peripubescent devolved Parliament, you might well reflect on the juxtaposition of emotive lines of belonging tattooed into the very flesh of the democratic body politic. Perhaps you read the last two visceral lines, 'flesh of my flesh and bone of my bone', puzzled at the evocative strength of feeling towards the writer's country and its public projection onto the building of a democratic parliament in a multicultural, left-of-centre nation whose sons and daughters contributed so greatly to rationalist Enlightenment thinking. Your brow furrows further, not least because you are now thinking far too hard for what was a bit of Edinburgh sightseeing, but more, now distracted from the pleasures of your leisure, you are troubled by your own banal invocation of the nation personified with tattooed flesh and sons and daughters as intellectual progeny. Possibly, though, you are more inclined to think that Gray's words hit the nail right on the head: they pretty much sum up how at times you feel about Scotland, or about some other country of which you are a son or daughter. You feel that this kind of emotive sentimentality, though firmly at home at an international football match, also feels appropriate enough for what was, fairly recently, a momentously new building and institution.

The establishment of the new devolved Parliament is a shibboleth for the political difference of Scotland within the Union, with a need to do things differently. Emblems, however, can have different meanings to different people and can be worn in any number of ways. Devolution has doubtlessly prompted interest in Scottish national identity as a subject for study, though interest in this so called 'stateless nation' pre-dates the establishment of the Parliament in 1999. Arguably, the modern chapter of Scottish national identity in political and cultural terms began in the 1960s with the rise of the Scottish National Party (SNP) as an electable political force, although the formation of the Union in 1707 and the following decades was fraught with tension (Devine 1999; Nairn 2000: 91–123) and opposition could be found 'at both the popular and elite levels' (Webb 1977: 47). It is because of such tension and oppositions that some trace the roots of contemporary nationalism to the very enactment of the Union, stressing the existence of an affirmative sense of Scottish national identity at the time (Bowie 2008), while others look at a variety of factors, including the decline of Empire and the social and industrial changes that asymmetrically beset Scotland as part of the UK (Nairn 1977; Pittock 2008). We consider the contemporary background to Scottish nationalism and national identity and its changing political context in more detail in Chapter 2, and our discussion reveals that there is now a significant body of theoretical and empirical work which has much to say about Scottish national identity although, of course, not all of it is of the same opinion.

Why, then, preface a discussion of the politics and discourse of Scottish national identity with a contrived thought experiment? Essentially, we mean to explore the relationship between Scottish national identity and Scottish politics. Implicitly presented above are two contrasting types of national identity: one closely allied to the perceived values of a democratic polity – open, pluralistic, civic and inclusive – while the other emanates from a place of bounded emotional belonging and ancestry – closed, homogeneous, non-civic and exclusive. These are important analytical distinctions (see Keating 2001) which, while often challenged as less than useful and dismissed as too general, allow for descriptions at various levels: descriptions of general theories of nationalism and national identity; descriptions of the nation as manifest in the private, public and political realms; and descriptions of academic discourse as it relates to the study of Scotland and Scottish national identity. There is far more here to drill down into, but in essence a re-examination of Scottish national identity and its corollary nationalism is proposed, one which looks specifically at the political dynamic with the wider public in which national identity occurs. In so doing, we cast our net widely in the sense of wishing to better understand the character of Scottish national identity, not only as a set of predetermined survey and interview questions but also as discourse at both mass and elite levels. The political is not just defined by and found in those civic and public institutions and the associated actions of individuals, though these are important, and so we seek to explore the (dis)connect between 'elite' political rhetoric and the wider mass realisations of national identity.

A note of caution about the use of terms: we make the contrast between civic and non-civic nationalism in that we use these terms as one way of describing aspects of Scottish nationalism and national identity. Also, at various times, we use the words ethnie, ethnic, ethnically, ethnicity and tribal. However, and let there be no mistake, we are not making a claim that Scottish national identity is predominantly a 'hot', ethnically based one, and the use of these words are at no time used as the ultra-perennialist simplisms of far-right Nationalist fantasists. Instead, we highlight that it is difficult, no matter how much one may wish, to get away from terms that denote belonging in less (rather than more) than rational and inclusive terms; and, further, to reduce the debate to bifurcations of 'rational' and 'irrational', 'civic' and 'non-civic' (and therefore 'good' versus 'bad') is to miss that these characteristics may be mutually supporting or at the very least co-extant. That said, we do prefer the more specific terms 'birthright' and 'ancestry' when indicating the specific non-civic and exclusive characteristics that can be identified in mass survey data, as it is these, rather than racial considerations, that can actually be evidenced. One final point on the term 'non-civic' is that in terms of the study of Scottish national identity it does not necessarily entail an exclusionary sense, which is explored more particularly in Chapter 4's analysis of the discursive drawing of Scotland by its politicians.

Whose Nationalism is it Anyway?

APPROACHES TO NATIONALISM

In historical terms, the modernism of nations has been well outlined by the likes of Renan (1990) or Hobsbawm (1990). Modern nation-states, it is claimed, are historically recent inventions, rising out of the old empires in the new capitalist economies, and more specifically through the occurrences of mass symbolic organisation evident in 'print capitalism' (Anderson 1983; and for an under-cited earlier example of this thesis McLuhan 1962). The symbolic qualities of national identities cannot be overlooked, as it is the means by which identities are projected, maintained and passed on, and by which nations are portrayed as ancient and perennial, even if they are not. The scholarly debate contains a mix of attitudes towards the symbols of Scottish identity, varying from describing them as symptomatic of a pathological malformation (Nairn 1977), parochial, atavistic and creatively empty signs (Craig 1982), being inconsequential to mass political behaviour (McCrone 2001) or defined as an essential othering from Anglo-Britishness (Ichijo 2004). There is an identifiable sense in much of this work that Scotland and its national identity are somehow unsatisfactory as a form of cultural life or even insubstantial to the business of politics. As Pittock has put it, 'One of the features of the creation of a Scottish cultural agenda after 1979 was a determination to rid the country of the historical clichés, inferiorism and misunderstandings which it was believed by some had held Scotland back from devolution' (2008: 123). Of course, Hobsbawm and Ranger's (1983) volume long ago disabused us of the folly of believing in the immutable and perennial existence of nations; clearly they are symbols that disingenuously reflect the realities they represent, as fantastic as the Sobieski forgeries which created them. Cairns Craig typifies this type of scholarly piety towards Scottish symbols of identity, in which 'Romantic glamour is an illusion in which the reason is suppressed by the power of the imagination in defiance of the best interests of humanity' (1982: 9). Overwhelmed by the larger, more powerful Anglo-British culture, which had more than a touch of its own rationalist, cosmopolitan glamour, nine-teenth-century authors such as Walter Scott and J. M. Barrie created foundation myths for an 'identity existing beyond history which could find its application at any particular moment and through any specific con-temporary situation: it was an identity lost and irrecoverable' (Craig 1982: 10). The nineteenth-century works of the Kailyard are literary fantasies whose readers are 'invited into a Scottish world only to have revealed its hollowness, its inadequacy to the complex reality of modern life' (Craig 1982: 9). So the story goes, denuded of the essential supporting role of its middle class, now committed to the cosmopolitan Anglo-British project, the myths, history and culture of Scotland become associated with atavism and provinciality.

This cultural legacy of the Kailyard is, according to Craig, profound and negative. Though commercially and internationally successful, the Kailyard for the individual writer 'established an image of Scotland as parochial and narrow-minded from which it has been hard to escape' (Craig 1982: 11). On a social level the impact is equally dramatic:

> The caricature, simplification and condescension of Kailyard writing are not merely literary styles, they are there to ensure that the author is seen, like middle-class Scotland in general, to be keeping his distance from a national identity from which he wished to be absolved. (Craig 1982: 11)

Scotland, through its artists, could no longer look forward and imagine a collective national future, for the past bears no resemblance to the present. The Tartanry and Kailyard now conceal the complexities of Scottish culture and history, papering over the cracks of suppressed rebellion and declining rural culture only to use the 'glassy essences' of those happenings as hidebound mythic symbols – Scotch mist, the noble savage and the 'lad o' pairts'. In the present we are left with inadequate and moribund husks of a mythic structure, leaving the modern artist only with symbolic tools from the past which are 'tainted, warped, blunted by the uses to which they have been put' (Craig 1982: 14–15). Colin McArthur agrees, arguing that in the realm of film 'powerful existing traditions of representation, or discourses, exist (as is the case with Scotland) even talented artists will find it extremely difficult to create representations outside the frameworks of these traditions' (1982: 65). As such these discourses 'within which Scotland and Scots have been represented in films have been wholly inadequate for dealing with the historical and contemporary reality of Scotland' (Craig 1982: 66).

If this rather bleak view of the symbolic apparatus of national identity, so irretrievably corrupted, is to be believed, how then did a distinctive sense of national identity survive in Scotland? Here the Edinburgh school of modernist thinkers have an answer: what mattered to the making and maintenance of Scots and Scotland was not a mawkish backward glance at the past but an autonomous civil society made up of an independent protestant church, autonomous local government and distinctively Scottish legal and educational systems (see Brown et al. 1996: 5 and Paterson 1994: 3–45). This local autonomy created a public space in which Scots could be Scots in their own way and it was a way cast in the mould of public-civic institutions. The result, according to those such as Keating (2001: 220), McCrone (2001) and Paterson (1999), was a form of national identity which is overwhelmingly civic rather than ethnic, *demos* rather than *ethnos*. This prompted Nairn to comment wryly, 'The Scots middle-class complex is of course rooted in the autonomous "civil society" bequeathed us by 1707. In this descriptive, and quite uncomplimentary, sense, we are too civil to be nationalistic' (Nairn 1997: 188) in the 'hot' Balkan sense of the term. So, in the modernist view, what does this civic nationalism consist of and what symbolic, cultural or historical resources does it draw on?

McCrone (2001) argues that we have to be cautious about Scottishness being the same through space and time, and that national identity is something that takes place through the social discourse of and on the issue of Scotland. There are links that can be made between the past and the present but one cannot consider being Scottish today and being Scottish in the fourteenth century as the same thing. The Scottish modernist would concur that history is a politically contested issue in the politics of Scottish identity, which works like *The Invention of Tradition* underscore. However, where history is drawn on in support of the modernist thesis it is used to support the ideas and ideals of inclusivity. The history that counts is the history of 'institutional autonomy' (Paterson 1994) and not some set of vague historic emotions. McCrone and others would stress the claim made by the Scottish writer William McIlvanney that the Scots are a 'mongrel nation' and echo the argument of Ferguson in that 'Scottishness was never exclusive, but on the contrary, has always been highly absorptive, a quality that it retains even in the vastly different circumstances of today' (Ferguson 1998: 305). Similarly, T. C. Smout (1969) is an historical resource drawn on to support the notion of Scottish identity as based on a 'sense of place' rather than a 'sense of tribe'. Therefore, with regard to the political deployment of history the Scottish modernists argue: 'Those who wish to argue that an ethnically diverse Scotland is the morally correct one are able to mobilise history to considerable effect' (McCrone 2001: 157).

Nairn's concept of 'neo-nationalism' as descriptive of the Scottish context has been taken up by Scottish focused modernists. This is a 'different and quite modern form of nationalism which cannot be accommodated or dismissed' (McCrone 2001: 189); it is different from nationalism in that it surfaces in states with well developed economies and from areas that, rather than being underdeveloped, are usually 'relatively advantaged'. The essential difference from, for example, former communist and Balkan countries, is that Scottish neo-nationalism is a progressive movement that stresses civic rather than ethnic features. It has an adaptable political ideology and built-in social democracy and neo-liberal aspects. This reflects a modernist interpretation of neo-nationalism as a positive socio-political force or identity. This stands in direct contrast to the depiction of 'unreconstructed', or 'traditional', nationalism as a negative identity or movement. Thus neo-nationalism, or civic nationalism, is both socially and politically acceptable, while ethnic, or non-civic, nationalism is exclusionary and unacceptable as either a social or a political movement.

McCrone states that the implications of this civic, democratic nationalism are that the primordialist foundations based on exclusion are not suited to 'a multicultural, interdependent world' and that 'Nationalist movements which take the regressive primordial route may flourish in the short term, but ultimately are doomed to fail' (2001: 188). Where culture is employed it is shown that Scotland and England are very similar, in many ways, and thus any claims on an identity basis must be political rather than cultural, or even ethnic, although such a claim directly contradicts the argument found among qualitative surveys that 'Scotland, according to Scottish nationalists, was, is and will always continue to be a nation, with a unique, identifiable culture' (Haesly 2005: 246).

Thus the Scottish modernist interpretation put forward is one of Scottishness as a territorial, civic-based form of identity, whereby an individual resident in Scotland can claim to be Scottish. Findings such as Haesly notwithstanding, there exists a considerable body of evidence on which this claim can be substantiated. First, voting in elections for the Scottish Parliament is based upon residence, which may be taken as support for this modernist position. Being a Scots-born individual resident elsewhere in the UK is not enough to vote for the Scottish Parliament; one must be resident in Scotland. Any British citizen living in Scotland can vote, irrespective of their sense of identity or ethnic basis. Of course, any European Union citizen living in Scotland can also vote in elections for the Scottish Parliament – as well as stand as a candidate for that institution. This simple fact has ramifications in any discussion on the nature of identity. The modernist position is supported by evidence based on ideas of citizenship rather than national belonging (an issue we take up in Chapter 5).

Second, this political aspect of Scottish identity is also said to be underlined by the comfort with which Scots negotiate a dual identity and remain British in significant numbers. Nor is there a simple relationship between national identity, political behaviour and constitutional preference. It is shown in any number of works that supporters of parties across the political spectrum choose the identity of Scottish before others (for instance, see Brown et al. 1998; Bond 2000; and Denver et al. 2000). There are SNP supporters who consider themselves primarily British and do not support independence, while at the same time a number of Labour supporters prefer independence as a constitutional option. What remains, and is perhaps even more valid a decade after devolution began, is that people in Scotland can clearly distinguish between their national (Scottish) and state (British) identities (Henderson 1999). People living in England, who consider themselves English/British do not easily make this state-nation distinction (McCrone 2001) but that is not to say that national identity does not matter to the English (McCrone and Bechhofer 2010). It seems that the issue of national and state identity is more complicated than considering these identities as the sides of a coin – at least for many individuals in different parts of the UK.

Third, some data moves the discussion beyond one of origin, birth and region into the area of race. Survey evidence drawn from studies among ethnic minorities living in Scotland indicates the existence of civic-inclusive characteristics to Scottish national identity. Many individuals within these communities, especially younger ones, are more likely to employ hybrid identifiers than their counterparts living in England, describing themselves as 'Scottish Muslim' or 'Scottish Pakistani', whereas English counterparts are more likely to identify with Britishness than Englishness (Hussein and Miller 2006).

What remains after these investigations is the existence of a sense of Scottish identity and the need to understand that identity in a political context. A simple correlation between party preference, constitutional preference, ethnic identity and national identity is not possible, but the need to understand the nature of that national identity becomes even more important. The understanding of that identity as a civic rather than ethnic form allows for a more benign understanding of the possible impact on the political and constitutional structure of Scotland and the UK. The basis for this, the overall modernist interpretation of Scottish nationalism as a civic form, is a cultural one. For McCrone and others being Scottish has become a stronger, and yet more culturally diverse, feeling in recent years. At the same time, Scotland and England are very similar in overall, general cultural terms. This, therefore, means that the emphasis on identity has to be political rather than cultural, and civic rather than ethnic (Keating 2001: 220). Thus the result is a sense of being Scottish that 'almost as a by-product, emphasises territorial inclusivity rather than ethnic inclusivity' (McCrone 2001: 177) and 'nationalist claims are based on . . . practical arguments about institutions, accountability and policy. This has made it one of the least romantic of nationalist movements.' (Keating 2001: 221).

However, this visibly modernist interpretation of Scottish national identity is not without its problems. It has tended to talk of 'nationalism' as something that political parties, and institutional elites in general, mobilise and pass down to the mass – a kind of 'caretaker' or 'pastoral' nationalism. The elite are the custodians of nationalist ideas – nation speaking unto nation – so that mass sentiment is usually framed in terms of measuring support for particular constitutional or policy preferences, as a means of describing them as distinctively Scottish, or not, as the case may be. This unquestionably has been a productive course of enquiry, particularly for empirically driven social science, allowing for mass surveys and measurement. However, the tendency has been to reduce the panorama within which national identity and nationalism can be seen, framing it ostensibly as elite, top-down and in the confines of public institutions.

In summation, there is a well-established narrative within the literature, exemplified here by Craig, characterising representations of a Scottish national culture post-1707 as parochial and wholeheartedly insufficient for 'proper' national discourse – which really means in the realms of high art, literature and culture with a big 'C'. Keating has described this as an 'inferiority complex' (2001: 230), whereby all that is progressive, modern and metropolitan is aligned with Britishness. Statements like 'Parochialism has indeed been a problem for Scottish cultural production' (Keating 2001: 230) are indicative of continuing rationalist, Enlightenment perspective (i.e. 'objective'), one that casts itself in the universal, outside of the hubbub of the cultural milieu. There appears to be two immediate problems with this position: first, statements like 'Parochialism has indeed been a problem' are rarely evidential or comparative in nature. The relative value of some particular cultural artefact or mode of production would engender the need to engage with types of aesthetic critique which 'objective' analysis feels better left to the Arts faculty, knowing well the ontologically shaky ground such subjective criticisms are built upon; they are not founded on the firmer ground of empirical evidence. Therefore, charges of inferiorism can be levelled with little need for eristic substantiation, and the likes of Craig and McArthur can be drawn upon when necessary. This raises the second problem: what are the comparative or qualitative criteria upon which charges of inferiorism are based? These charges have more than a ring of cultural elitism and the circularity of a self-fulfilling prophecy about them. Everything British, metropolitan and progressive is good; everything else is provincial and consequently bad. The relative value of any particular cultural artefact seems inherently defined by the power relations operating within the context of its cultural production and consumption (Bourdieu 1991). As Billig (1995) has already noted, academics cannot remove themselves from the cultural and discursive production of nations. The Scottish modernist tradition, discussed latterly, has tended to concentrate on the 'rational', civic-institutional aspects of Scottish nationalism, whilst leaving the wider aspects of Scottish private and public cultural life untouched, including not regarding their own articulations as indicative of a variety of elite cultural production. Academics, just as artists, journalists and everyone else, are inculcated in the discursive and cultural production of nations. Pittock provides a useful explanation of this strand of Scottish scholarly critique in relation to the wider cultural *habitus*:

> demythologizers of the 1980s and '90s pursued the work of their Enlightenment predecessors, whom they saw themselves as transcending, in imposing moral categories on the Scottish past to justify a judgement on it. Tartanry was to be as inferior, false and misleading as Jacobitism once had been: and the supreme irony of these decades was that just as academics and cultural commentators lamented the meretriciousness of tartan and shortbread images of their country, the kilt and all its associated furniture of stereotype were being increasingly adopted by young people as a mark of vibrant, modern Scotland. In the 1970s and even the '80s, getting married or attending formal occasions in a kilt was far less common than it is today, and many who wore it wore it as a badge of belonging to a caste in society rather than simply the visible performance of being a Scot, which is what it has now become. While the academy practised postmodern theorizing combined with a naive allegiance to the 'facts' of Scottish history and culture, Scottish society was increasingly being performed by those able to revisit the past without irony in order to show their commitment to the present. We all have our myths, and it turned out that 'Scotch myths' are no worse than anyone else's. (Pittock 2008: 123)

Stories of a rational, civic, and pluralistic nationalism, the inheritance of the Scottish Enlightenment and Scotland's commitment to the cosmopolitan Anglo-British project are still stories being told to satisfy particular mores and desires – the desire to be seen as rational, civic-minded and cosmopolitan, for instance. On what basis is the value of these civic stories greater than other 'Scotch myths', other than through the subjective ascriptions of cultural authorities?

AN ALTERNATIVE PERSPECTIVE

Of course another reading of Scottish national identity is possible. Nairn, for example, while committed to the modernism of nations and the role of civic institutions in the cultural production of Scottish nationalism, has also noted a 'tenacious popular memory':

> From the time of Walter Scott onwards, these roots of statehood were endowed with the glamour of a lost kingdom, and the tantalizing sense of redemption which always informs nostalgia. Although mocked from the outset as wilful and unreasonable, this display-identity has in truth proved incomparably stronger than every one of its philistine adversaries. Colonial empire, Liberalism, the heavy-industrial workshop of the world, British Socialism and Thatcherism have all in turn become as Nineveh and Tyre; while the eclipsed state-land of the Scots has run beneath and outlasted each ruin in turn, until ready to resume its interrupted existence. (Nairn 2000: 12–13)

In Nairn's variation on the reading of post-1707 what was left of the apparatus of state in Scotland could not be considered at all insubstantial: 'it can't be said that everything left in national hands was "low" or less dignified, since 1707's "Devolution" included the care of souls'. The establishment of the Church of Scotland ensured 'a national stamp upon the heavens as well as on the parish pump' so that at 'that time the de-stratified Scots were urged to be content with true piety and the afterlife; now they are encouraged to keep out of trouble by indulging in the secular cultivation of literature and the arts' (Nairn 2000: 97).

Moving further away from modernist territory into ethno-symbolism, Ichijo echoes this idea of a disjunction between an elite and mass interpretation of history and culture: 'Despite the official denunciation of the Scottish past, the Scots continued to cherish their memories of Wallace and Bruce, Robert Burns, the Jacobite myth, and their tradition of the "Lad o' Pairts" even after the Union of 1707' (2004: 155). She also asserts that the 'Scottish have a long history and their historical memory is rich', not merely limited to the modernist period and the time since the Union, one rich with heroes and heroines, ancient monarchical blood lines and 'golden ages – the reigns of Alexander and Robert I, the Enlightenment, the age of improvement – as well as the myths of "Red Clyde" and militant socialism' (Ichijo

2004: 150). Such approaches argue for the inclusion of history and the acceptance of a longer existence of the nation than modernists would allow.

We employ such an approach in this book; one that could be labelled as an ethno-symbolist perspective. While a basic argument of this approach is that nations, and their formation, should be examined over an historically protracted period (*la longue durée*) and that the emergence of modern nations cannot be understood without considering the various ethnic groups that have gone before, we do not carry out such a study here. Such studies have been undertaken, examining the history of Scotland, with the union, nationalism and national identity as core themes (see Harvie 1977 and Devine 2008 as examples). Rather, we are concerned with the contemporary political aspects and implications, an area that ethno-symbolism has not traditionally addressed and for which it has, rightly, been criticised (Guibernau 1999).

The criticism levelled against the ethno-symbolist approach is that nations and nationalism did not exist before the modern era (Özkirimli 2010). This is, of course, a keystone of a modernist critique and yet it is used in reverse to criticise critics of the approach: by stressing only the modern features of nationalism modernists ignore other historical evidence. As can be seen by his comments and critiques on modernism Anthony D. Smith represents a halfway house between primordialism and modernism (1998). National identity must be seen as a cultural and collective phenomenon (thus agreeing with Anderson), yet Smith dismisses Hobsbawm's contention that nationalism is mere invention (1991). Smith freely admits that nations are a modern phenomenon but argues that they incorporate features from the *ethnies* and previous eras (1986). In other words, history is important to an understanding of nationalism and national identity in the modern context, the recycling and reinterpretation of historical narratives, figures and other iconography (for an illustration of reinvention and vacilating uses of Britannia, Boadicea and John Bull through time see Dresser 1989 and Surel 1989).

An ethno-symbolic approach accepts that myths and symbols are subjectively interpreted, but not that they are 'constructed' in the pejorative sense of the term. Instead, a national mythology is drawn from the past and the history of the peoples in question. While elites and others may attempt to interpret such material to further their particular cause, they are constrained in their use of them by the historical legacy of the group in question (see R. Smith 2003 and Ichijo 2004). One can present William Wallace and Rob Roy as nationalist heroes fighting the English, and this may or may not be the actuality of who they were, but neither is an invention. Both are important cultural symbols, and cannot be dismissed as unimportant, nor can they be presented outside of a limited range. Any attempt to alter history too much is met with resistance from members of the group to whom that history 'belongs'. Mythological heroes may have been bandits but any attempt to change the public perception of such heroes is difficult, as those wishing to employ particular narratives for political purposes must do so within a symbolic repertoire accessible to those they wish to persuade (Hutchinson 2008 and R. Smith 2003).

We have been knowingly utilising language in this introduction that infers the significance of symbolic and discursive recourses to both the studies and manifestations of nationalism and national identity. Michael Billig and Benedict Anderson, perhaps above all others, have made the most original and eloquent exposition of the discursive qualities of nations and their nationalisms, and it is an approach firmly integrated into our study. Reflecting on his motivation for writing, and the impact of *Imagined Communities*, Anderson commented, 'the book attempted to combine a kind of historical materialism with what later on came to be called discourse analysis' (2006: 227). Both Anderson and Billig are essentially 'texualists', in Ong's sense of the term (1982: 165–70), in that their approaches to nationalism are based on an interest in the instrumental influence of printed texts (rather than oral-aural aspects of language) to affect consciousness and thereby impinge on material reality. Texts from this point of view are not merely artefacts but sites of social interaction and creation. Texts, therefore, are dialectical and socially constitutive: writer, audience and context are iteratively constructed (Bourdieu 1991; Fairclough 1992, 2001; and Swales 1990). For both Billig and Anderson the press and 'the novel' are of principal importance to an investigation of nations and nationalisms because they are orientated to specific, situated audiences which co-locate the nation, the state and society (MacInnes et al. 2007). Anderson focused more on 'the novel', while Billig's concern in *Banal Nationalism* was the popular daily print press. For Anderson the two modes of novels and the print press 'provide the technical means for "re-present-ing" the *kind* of imagined community that is the nation' (2006: 25 original emphasis). And both these modes, though in existence before, 'flowered in Europe in the eighteenth century' (Anderson 2006: 24–5), tallying well with the modernist timings of nationalism.

Anderson's thesis is premised on an account of what he influentially termed 'print capitalism', whereby the possibility of the mass imagining of nations is made possible through the consumption of industrial printing by the readers of regionalised vernaculars (see McLuhan 1962). The capital of the printed word ushers in the possibility of a new collective psychological condition, where widespread literacy signals a deep interiorisation of the vernacular printed word. Novels and newspapers facilitated 'the imagination of national communities in two ways: contributing to a sense of temporal synchronicity through reproducing a sense of empty world time, and promoting an illusory simultaneity of experience' (MacInnes et al. 2007: 188). Though disconnected and spread over a wide geographical area, peoples could imagine themselves as coterminous because the manifold exactitude of mechanical printing enabled, created a market for, and consequently institutionalised, their shared spoken language (or at least a dialect more intelligible to them than Latin), freeing these languages from their immediate spoken contexts. Be they in Aberdeen or Irvine, readers of *Trainspotting* can imagine fellow readers elsewhere reading exactly the same words.

Novels and the popular print press are important for other reasons too. The novel has been a site of significant intellectual and artistic expression; it is the 'form in which Western culture since the Enlightenment has most notably conducted the education and examination of feeling' (Bell 1990: 196). Literature continues to be a site of high art, critical reflection and mass consumption, and, as our discussion of the Kailyard above indicates, perhaps also low art and uncritical sentimental consumption. The press's Habermasian role in the public debate of democratic life continues to hold currency. In a modern Scotland Higgins noted that 'the importance of the Scottish media has resided in its presenting one of the best-established ways in which "Scots" can participate in being Scottish' (2004b: 634). Therefore, the press and 'the novel' are significant sites for public expression of the self and society.

Though Billig and Anderson are both important and influential in the studies of nations and nationalism, their accounts are not without difficulties. At their heart the difficulties lie in what they conceive 'the novel' and a national print press to be like. In short, Anderson envisages a totalised imagining of the national community in what he, tongue in cheek, calls the performative of the 'daily plebiscite'. For Billig too the nation is manifest in the daily routine of forgotten remembrance of the national *habitus*, utilising Bourdieu's metaphor of embodied social life. These are monolithic, centripetal views of national discourse (or rather of the nation constituted through discourse), unifying audiences into homogeneous, standardised national continuities, and limiting the possibilities available to mass social imaginings. Both the nation and its modes of representation are, conceptually and in analytical practice, singular unities.

The problem, therefore, with these unifying conceptions is that the national audiences which they are said to comprise are in reality multi-faceted (Bhabha 1990; MacInnes et al. 2004). This criticism is similar to the one levelled above at modernist approaches though in neither approach is the method they use implicated in this criticism, and as such we draw heavily on both traditions here under the ontological point of view of ethno-symbolism.

METHODOLOGY

As can be seen from our discussion, our study of national identity and politics in Scotland employs a mixed-method approach, stretching across traditions and disciplines. A combination of empirical political science, content analysis, qualitative interviews and linguistically based discourse analysis are used to explore the similarities and differences between elite political instantiations of national identity and those manifest in discourse and opinions of the wider public. Among the specific issues that we will focus upon are the varying emphases within the political arena in terms of national identity, nationalism and political alignment, and the changing nature of that sense of identity as employed by the major political parties. We shall focus on the manifestos produced specifically for Scotland at British General Elections since the 1970s. These key historical and core political documents have received extremely limited attention and have never before been subject to any rigorous, codified measurement, an oversight we address here. We shall also consider individual political elite conceptions through interviews with Members of Parliament (MPs) elected from Scotland and Members of the Scottish Parliament (MSPs). This aspect of our research allows for an analysis of how these political actors perceive Scottish national identity and the Scottish nation, seeking to build upon our understanding of the overall party positions within Scotland. However, we offset this strong elite focus with a consideration of national identity from below. In too many academic considerations of nationalism and national identity, the focus has been on either a purely elite conception of these phenomena, or the informative, yet still somewhat limited, statistical analysis of mass study data to gain insights from members of the nation. We fully employ such data within this work, allowing us to consider the construction and understanding of national identity at the mass level, yet we also support and expand our analysis with an examination of how members of the wider public elucidate their individual national identity in an everyday setting.

Specifically we seek to illustrate the existence of disconnect between the elite and, in the language of political science, the mass of the Scottish nation. Our object is not to demonstrate what Scottish nationalism 'really' consists of; rather we believe that there is a plurality of Scottish national identities and that while there are locations of convergence between elite and mass versions there is also divergence. Particularly, we wish to challenge the notion that Scottish nationalism is of an overwhelmingly civic, open and pluralistic type; but that equally does not mean that it is 'hot', irrational and bigoted. Rather, there is a far more delicate interplay between what can be categorised as civic and open forms and non-civic and closed forms of Scottish nationalism.

As Henderson (2007) suggests, any methodological outline, especially one addressing a study of national identity and nationalism, struggles with the issue of terminology. Throughout the book we, as did she in her comparative analysis of Scotland and Quebec, employ the term 'nationalist' with regard to those individuals and political parties that, through language or behaviour, seek to maintain or strengthen the political position of Scotland. The term 'unionist' describes those parties seeking to maintain the existence of the United Kingdom as a state. However, as we shall see, all political parties in Scotland operate within a nationalist framework and all employ nationalist language to a greater or lesser degree; therefore, nationalist and nationalism with a small 'n' refers to the political behaviour of all major parties in Scotland, whilst Nationalists with a capital 'N' refers only to parties who seek a fully independent Scotland, i.e. the SNP. One of the major contributions that this work makes to the study of nationalism in Scotland is the introduction of means by which the position of the parties can be measured on a nationalist–unionist axis, but being pro-union does not make a party anti-Scotland. Far from it: unionist arguments for Scotland's continued incorporation within the UK state are made in the 'interest' of Scotland and as such are nationalist with a small 'n'.

OVERVIEW

As indicated, this study is largely comparative, beginning with an examination of elite political expressions of nationalism. The contemporary period since the 1970s is our main focus, and so the following chapter examines events from that period in more detail, drawing attention to the wider socio-political context of the politics of nationalism in Scotland. Elite political discourse is then dealt with in three further chapters. The manifesto content analysis of Chapter 3 indicates the changing employment of a sense of Scottish identity in the central campaigning documents of mainstream politics, particularly in relation to the congruent British identity. Billig's 'banal' thesis is revisited in Chapter 4 through the linguistic phenomenon of metaphor. Here the banal reference to the nation as a personified individual is explored to demonstrate discursively how the elite characterise the national body in all the same ways in which individual members of the nations can be described: not just rational but also emotional, not just open and pluralistic but also particularistic and unique. This discourse analysis is repeated on non-elite discourse two chapters later in the narrative storytelling of contributors to an online discussion of a national newspaper article, illustrating the differing types of stories individuals use in the construction of personal national identities. The masses' perception is further discussed through the re-examination of mass survey data from the last four decades, and here in particular we meet the Scottish modernists on their own territory, questioning some interpretations of the data which has previously been offered. The study finishes by returning to elite discourse but this time instead of scrutinising some particular genre of communication we have interviewed members of the Scottish political elite on the issue of Scottish national identity and nationalism.

2

The Politics of Contemporary Scottish Nationalism

For nationalism to become a major political movement, it requires the masses to engage with the idea of being members of a nation and to form a polity, or part of it. Nationalism is a community of the mind (Anderson's (1983) 'imagined community') linking together individuals sharing the same belief in membership of a national community. If political nationalism is to have any chance of success the masses must be engaged with the political system. Although there is clear evidence of nationalist activity and intent, including declarations in support of Scottish independence or home rule, prior to the emergence of mass politics within the UK many of the organisations involved lacked a mass connection. Even when mass politics began to emerge within the UK the extension of the franchise to all males over twenty-one and to most women over thirty was not in place until 1918, and it was only with the 1929 election that both genders achieved franchise parity. Furthermore, because of the widespread economic crises of the 1930s and the Second World War, it was not until the 1945 election that a clear partisan choice was available to the Scottish (and British) electorate, when all four major parties of the latter twentieth century were present, albeit that the presence of the SNP was very limited'.[1] Therefore, we argue that an explicit age of nationalist and mass engaged politics in Scotland did not begin until the end of the Second World War.

In addition, 1945 was the year in which Scottish political nationalism first victoriously asserted itself when the SNP won a by-election in Motherwell. In a straight two-way fight with Labour (as the Liberals and Conservatives did not field candidates because of a wartime agreement), the SNP took 51.4 per cent of the vote. Although the SNP lost the seat at a General Election

---

[1] In 1945 the SNP stood eight candidates, a number it would not again surpass until the 1964 General Election.

only three months later, they maintained some local standing and pushed the Conservatives into third place. Those three short months heralded the possibility of a new age in Scottish politics. For the first time, the SNP had tasted electoral victory and became committed to maintaining a strong focus on elections (Lynch 2002). The party committed to the idea of Scottish independence had been represented in the Commons. A milestone was reached, but it would prove to be an isolated marker which would not be repeated for another forty-two years.

Despite our assertion outlined above, nationalism itself is not a recent aspect of the Scottish socio-political arena and should not be considered a purely twentieth-century phenomenon. The presence of Scottish nationalism together with nationalist organisations and ideals prior to and during the eighteenth and nineteenth centuries has been widely discussed (for example, Harvie 1998; Morton 1999). Latent examples of nationalist emphasis are evident in such historical documents as the 1320 Declaration of Arbroath (Cowan 2003). The presence of nationalist intent can be obviously recognised in the activities of such organisations as the National Association for the Vindication of Scottish Rights (founded 1853) or the Scottish Home Rule Association (founded 1886). The idea of Scotland having a parliamentary assembly has been mooted for much of the period since 1707 when the Scottish Parliament voted itself out of existence, along with the English Parliament, and the British Parliament was initiated.[2] There was a firm Scottish nationalism present in the late nineteenth century, albeit one allied to the idea of Union (Morton 1999). The British state was attentive to such feelings and created the Scottish Office in 1885. The office of Secretary of State for Scotland followed shortly thereafter, although it was dismissed as somewhat 'low status' (McGarvey and Cairney 2008). This nonetheless helped to maintain the conduit between what were, at that time, fairly autonomous institutions of Scotland and the central government of the UK.

Such activity notwithstanding, Scottish and British politics lacked an organised and electorally effective nationalist political party for much of the twentieth century. It was not until 1934 that the Scottish Party and the National Party of Scotland came together to form the SNP, which is currently the most pedigreed of pro-independence parties. However, both of those founding organs of the SNP were relatively young. The National Party of Scotland had only formed in April 1928 as an amalgam of four separate

---

[2] Ichijo argues, however, that while the Scottish Parliament did vote to dissolve, the 'English parliament was refashioned as the British parliament' (Ichijo and Spohn 2005: 20).

organisations; the Scottish Party was a more right wing, 'establishment-minded' organisation that only emerged in 1932 (Finlay 2009). The merger removed the possibility of competing nationalist candidates at by-elections, which was a key element behind the push to unite the two parties (Brand 1978; Harvie and Jones 2000). The SNP remained a fringe party, with little electoral impact and a very limited record of success. It would be another forty years before the party would become a regular aspect of day-to-day Scottish/British politics, and it is argued that it was not until the advent of devolution that it became part of the political mainstream (Mitchell 2009).

Nonetheless, while nationalism may have appeared politically quiescent and very peripheral until the mid to late 1960s, it should not be dismissed, because it was very much an aspect of Scottish politics and society. Whatever the level of support in Scotland for any form of devolution, a strong sense of Scottish national identity has always been present. While the latter part of the twentieth century has witnessed significant political, social and economic change, a continuing sense of national identity has remained. The idea of being Scottish and the idea of Scotland as a distinct nation has always informed and impacted upon political events. As this chapter will demonstrate, even when the SNP was a fringe party with little obvious public support and even less electoral impact, the idea of Scottish home rule/devolution was never far from the public imagination. When the SNP emerged as a more palpable political force and began regularly to attract significant minority support from the Scottish electorate, other political parties, especially the two major parties that alternately controlled Westminster, addressed the issue of Scotland and devolution more clearly and began to deliver a variety of measures. These measures ranged from minor symbolic actions to major constitutional proposals, the ramifications of which have yet to be fully realised.

The major parties of British politics, Conservative and Labour, perceived the SNP as a threat to their respective political fortunes in Scotland[3] and undertook activity to halt the increasing expression of support to the SNP at election time. However, such action could only take place because of the existence of an underlying assumption that Scotland was different and that Scottish solutions, rather than British solutions, were required. For any form of devolution to take place, a sense of nationalism and national identity had to be present. Even in the absence of an electorally effective pro-independence party, Scotland never suffered from a lack of identity. For political changes to occur, alongside altering party fortunes, the need for

---

[3] Wales was also a consideration for both the major British parties, as the Welsh nationalist party Plaid Cymru was emerging at the same time as the rise of the SNP in Scotland.

change in the social realm and between individuals and the state were required. The SNP was 'in the right place at the right time, making explicit, as well as problematic, the "national" dimension of the post-war consensus, and providing a political alternative when the British settlement began to fail" (McCrone 2001: 118).

The main aim of this chapter is to demonstrate the presence of a continual sense of Scottish identity in Scotland during the latter part of the twentieth century and how this impacted upon Scottish politics. We will begin by highlighting the major social changes that Scotland has undergone, and then consider interrelated trends evident in Scottish politics since 1945 through an analysis of General Election results. These include the decline of the Conservative and Unionist Party, the domination of Labour in post-war Scottish politics, the resurgence of the Liberal/Liberal Democrats and the rise of the SNP as an electoral force. These developments become evident in any analysis of Scottish electoral behaviour at British General Elections and have been well analysed (see, for example, Bennie et al. 1997; Brown 1999; McCrone 2001). We shall also then consider the electoral results for Scottish Parliament elections.

However, in order to place our analysis within the wider political context, some of the major non-parliamentary and political activity that has taken place in Scotland over the past sixty years, such as the Scottish Covenant of the 1940s and 50s, the reaction of Labour and the Conservatives to the rise of the SNP, the 1978 referendum in Scotland, the Constitutional Convention of the 1980s and 90s, and the subsequent 1997 referenda, are also discussed.

THE SCOTTISH COVENANT AND THE 1950S

It was not in the realm of electoral politics that the presence of a strong sense of Scottishness was found during the middle of the twentieth century. The SNP remained a very limited organisation, only one part of a wider nationalist movement (Hanham 1969). This reflects the fact that home rule, devolution and independence were not and are still not the sole preserve of the SNP (McGarvey and Cairney 2008). Many organisations could be included under the national movement heading, either small in terms of membership, or specific in geographic organisation. Some had significant effects on the SNP or provided for greater socio-political expression of Scottish national identity than either elections or political parties, with perhaps the most important of these being the Scottish Convention and the associated Covenant Association.

The Scottish Convention was born out of a major split in the nationalist ranks and leadership in 1942. Over half the membership of the SNP departed and while the end result was a smaller and much more ideologically focused party, it was politically even weaker. As a pressure group, the Scottish Convention was a cross-party and organisation platform with little working-class support (Brand 1978). The most important contribution the organisation made to the national movement was through their non-electoral activity, the clearest example being the Scottish National Assembly, the inaugural meeting which was held in 1947. The main outcome of the Assembly was the idea of the National Covenant. The Covenant was introduced at a meeting in Edinburgh in October 1949, where 1,200 delegates from across the national movement, including the SNP, signed the initial document. Purposefully echoing the language of the seventeenth-century religious covenant that established the rights of the Church of Scotland, the 1950 document was a petition to Westminster in which signatories committed themselves to the establishment of a Scottish parliament within 'the framework of the United Kingdom'.

The response from the Scottish public was immediate. Over 50,000 had signed the document within a week, and it became clear that public support was much higher than expected (Hanham 1969), which was likely a delight to the Association. A shortage in supply of documents for people to sign quickly became a problem, illustrating that the National Covenant was 'a popular and exciting project married to an inability to organise or follow through on anything like the same scale' (Brand 1978: 246). The actual number who signed the National Covenant has long been a bone of contention. Some estimates place the figure at over two million. However, verification of signatures was problematic, and Harvie and Jones (2000) and others (for example, Brand 1978; Hanham 1969; Lynch 2002) indicate that many fictitious names were present.

Whatever the actual number of signatures collected, the reaction of the Labour Government was firmly negative (as was that of the Conservatives), and the impact of the Covenant in immediate political terms was limited. The 1950 and 1951 election results (see Table 2.1) demonstrate that voter intent did not mirror claims made by supporters of home rule. Although 1951 saw the formal creation of the Scottish Covenant Association, which would soldier on until the early 1960s, such activity followed 'a tried, tested and failed approach' (Mitchell 1996: 97).

Nonetheless, the Covenant Movement was important to Scottish nationalism in two distinct ways (Brand 1978). First, it acted as a stepping stone which drew many people into the wider nationalist movement and from there into the SNP ranks, which it had initially overshadowed (Lynch 2002). Second, by raising awareness of the debate about Scotland, the Covenant publicly emphasised the idea of Scotland as a distinct nation with a sense of national destiny and rights. A large number of individuals within Scotland signed the Covenant, and regardless of the ambiguities surrounding the intent of the document or the exact meaning of home rule, a significant number of Scots held a strong sense of their national identity. The Covenant indicated the strength of that national feeling. The wording of the document which so many signed made it quite clear that, while the 1950s was the period of Unionist electoral hegemony within Scotland and the Covenant supporters pledged themselves to operate within the framework of the UK ('in all loyalty to the Crown'), they were also indicating support for a legislative authority that would operate in Scotland on Scottish affairs.

Another group within the nationalist movement that was active during the 1950s was the Scottish National Convention (SNC). The head of the SNC had recently been President of the SNP and ran the organisation while still a party member, even though the SNC rivalled the SNP in many ways. The SNC acted as an umbrella group; within its ranks were such organisations as the Scottish Socialist Party (not directly related to the present-day entity of the same name) and the Scottish Patriots. The SNP prohibited party members from affiliation with the organisation in the late 1950s when its activities began to disturb the leadership (Brand 1978). At that time the SNC began to decline because of its failure to carve out a role for itself or to further nationalist objectives.

The SNP made the declaration of prohibition because it had begun to see the SNC as a political embarrassment. During the twentieth century, many organisations that existed in the greater national movement operated in a manner that the SNP deemed politically damaging to the cause of Scotland for several reasons. The national movement may have come together under the SNP banner in the 1930s, but several other organisations have continued to spring up and then disappear. These groups often had very little appeal, usually being associated with either one individual or one particular area. More recent examples include Settler Watch and Siol nan Gaidheal during the 1970s and 1980s. While the Covenant Association and the SNC (albeit an umbrella group that included some fairly peripheral organisations) were general exceptions to that rule, they still ultimately suffered as a result of their limited support or achievements.

Many of the individuals who attracted support for and from the national movement were figures who had been expelled or had resigned from the SNP (a tradition that continues through to our times, as one of the most publicly recognisable Scottish nationalists, Margo MacDonald, sits as an independent MSP, having been expelled from the party in 2003). Many of them had often been active among the wider national movement and were somewhat extreme in their views or unwilling to adapt to the electoral avenue. Many went on to form more mainstream, but no more successful, organisations such as the SNC or the SCA; others remained very much on the political fringe and engaged in activities and organisations that brought little to the national movement in terms of support. As far as the SNP was concerned, these newly formed organisations were 'extremely unwelcome' (Lynch 2002: 72).

Wendy Wood was one such individual and remained a very colourful figure within the nationalist movement for several decades. Among the various organisations in which she was involved were the Scottish Patriots (part of the SNC while it existed) and the Democratic Scottish Self-Government Organisation. She was a forceful and able public speaker (Brand 1978) and a media darling in her own right (Hanham 1969). However, she very much represented the fringe aspect of the national movement, one that the SNP at the time did not find suitable (and nor does it still) in attempting to convey their message as a serious political party aiming for Scottish independence. It may well be that Wood was cut from old-style cloth, that of the national movement organisations of the early twentieth century, with too much romanticism and not enough political acumen, but she 'constituted a less toxic version of the grandes dames of Irish Nationalism . . . and no demonstration was complete without her green cloak. But in the 1950s this romanticism served to underline the forlornness of the Scottish cause' (Harvie and Jones 2000: 68).

The problems that the SNP, and other aspects of the wider national movement, had with such individuals or organisations was the nature of their message and the manner in which that message was delivered. The SNP increasingly sought to convey the nationalist cause more broadly than the need for self-representation for its own sake. Many organisations, such as the Scottish Patriots, presented a less politically and electorally acceptable face of Nationalism, which was and is still seen by the political elite as negative and reactionary. The SNP, which saw itself as the mainstream party of Scottish Nationalism, argued for a more positive and forward-looking ideal, which it has only emphasised more during the last few decades (Leith 2008). It sought to develop itself in terms of political identity and electoral coherence (Finlay 2009). Other organisations provided social and electoral drag on the development of a mainstream nationalist movement and a source of attack and ridicule from political opposition and unfriendly media.

Ultimately, the 1950s represented a low point in electoral and political achievements for the overall national movement. Without doubt, there was a strong national identity, held by a large number of Scots at that time. Individual Scots had joined together in a public expression of nationhood and pledged themselves to a Scottish parliament as well as a strong sense of nation. The Covenant was an act beyond that of a banal or habitual performative of nationalism. Signing the document required a conscious articulation which recognised and accepted an existing national identity. During the next few decades, Scotland would undergo significant change that would revolutionise Scottish politics and society, but the Scottish Covenant episode illustrates that such changes did not result in the emergence of a strong sense of Scottish national identity or the idea that Scotland should have a parliament/assembly; these ideas were already part of the social and political make-up of Scotland.

SOCIAL CHANGE IN SCOTLAND

The years following 1945 saw significant changes in many areas, economic, social and political. Changes included the diminution of heavy industry, the rise of a service-oriented sector, the changing role of women in society (and politics), the massive enlargement of the welfare state and major growth in higher education. These changes have impacted upon Scotland and have been considered in a recent work (Pittock 2008) that illustrates their importance in relation to both identity and politics in Scotland. Most importantly, from our perspective, these changes provided political opportunity to the SNP (Finlay 2009).

In considering Scotland, Murray Pittock (2008) provides a clear and cogent analysis that highlights the changes that impacted all sections of Scottish society. Focusing on post-1960s Scotland, he considers the general picture from the election of the Labour Government in 1945. Primarily, Pittock highlights what he sees as the 'mixed blessing' of government action – where major policy-making decisions tended towards centralisation (as in a British view), but also included Scottish-focused policies and distinct areas within Scotland. It is the contradiction in such plans, between the central and the local (or national in this case), that he considers as one of the major problems Scotland faced. Scotland suffered by having policies that were created and controlled centrally but that were impacted by the distorting factor of the Scottish Office, which operated policies specifically for Scotland.

For the last forty years, Scotland's GDP has been low when compared to other areas of the UK, and other EU countries, and it has suffered from a number of central initiatives that 'have failed to take lasting root' (Cuthbert and Cuthbert 2009: 106). Any economic advantages to the Union may well 'have been exhausted' (Keating 2009) as the major industries of Scotland have disappeared. Pittock argues that such decline can be tied to the social decline that has taken place in Scotland, resulting in an identity problem for the nation. Certainly, the social relationships in Scotland have undergone significant change (Paterson et al. 2004) during the past few decades and changing social relationships have resulted in a 'reframing of the political agenda' (Keating 2009: 53).

Such arguments highlight one of the major themes that have been employed to examine the rise of nationalism and devolution as a theme of Scottish politics: the end of Empire. Scotland benefited from the Empire in more ways than one. It had produced an outlet for those who sought employment outside of Scotland and provided a basis for career-minded individuals from the middle classes. The removal of these outlets only weakened the attraction of Empire and the Union (Marquand 1997). Such conjecture is not surprising. As society shapes the national perception, any impact upon social structures and organisation must likewise impact upon identity. Scotland, long an important player within global affairs (through the Empire), had considered itself to be a 'mother-nation' of that Empire. Yet the decline of Empire corresponded with a decline of industry. As the shipyards, coalmines, car plants and steel mills closed, a significant aspect of Scottish identity, identified by Hague as 'Clydesidism' (1994), was no longer recognisable. The economic powerhouse, the 'engine of Empire', had ceased to exist. Nairn argued that that the end of Empire will result in the end of Britain (1977), although such a purely instrumental interpretation of Britishness has been strongly challenged (Aughey 2010).

The idea of decline, occurring in such a manner as to affect the nature of Scottish identity, is not limited to purely economic matters and has also been linked to the Church of Scotland (Pittock 2008). The Kirk is always documented as one of the pillars that served to continue Scottish identity (Brand 1978; Lynch 2002). Pittock argues that the importance of the Church of Scotland has fallen as Scottish society has, like many European societies, become much more secular. Alongside the lessening of the role of the Kirk and Presbyterianism in general has been the changing role of the Catholic Church in Scotland (Devine 1999; 2008). Like other Christian denominations, the Catholic Church has seen its numbers decline, but it seems to have adopted the role of 'major clerical voice in Scotland' (Pittock 2008: 51) and its number of adherents allows it to challenge the Church of Scotland for that role. Consequently, this has allowed for a significant change in Scottish identity. Pittock argues that as 'Orange manifestations' have disappeared, there has been a growing interest in culture and history, much of which was for so long disapproved of in Presbyterian circles. Furthermore, the sectarianism prevalent in some aspects of Scottish society has dwindled, and this has had further consequences for Scottish society and identity. Such change has had clear political consequences: Catholics can now connect with the SNP and see that party as a viable voting vehicle; this has been a noticeable trend in recent years.

In short, Pittock makes clear that 'Scotland, then, has changed substantially since 1945, more particularly from 1960' (2008: 52). His analysis allows us to highlight the overarching nature of change and the fact that the political change discussed here has not taken place in a vacuum. However, the resulting changes of connectivity that have emerged from the transformations in Scottish society are equally important. The importance of the Union, and the benefits it brings, have become more open to question in Scotland (Mitchell 1996). The identity connections that Scotland formed as a result of the importance of Clydesidism in the west of Scotland have gone, and a new connectivity has emerged in their place. The essence of Pittock's argument is that he considers the British elements that one can find in Scottish society to be recent additions, the result of the centralising policies which resulted in a lessening of the autonomous nature of Scotland and the imposition of control from the centre. This clearly challenged the relationship that Scottish nationalism had with the Union during the preceding century (Morton 1999). Even while this control was mitigated by the activity of the Scottish Office, whose financial power and organisational authority was clear in the 1980s (Kellas 1989), Scotland operated on an administrative form of devolution with strong central control, thereby feeding political claims for 'Scottish answers to Scottish problems'.

Pittock stresses that 'social organisation, the pattern of industry, housing, religion, and education differs significantly in Scotland' (2008: 52). It is just as important to note that even where the differences between Scotland and other parts of the UK are minimal they are, in the Scottish mind's eye, larger, and this tendency has been more pronounced in recent years as divergences have become more visible. The election of the Thatcher Government in 1979 and the subsequent Conservative victories saw markedly different voting in Scotland and England. The policies of Thatcherism were not popular in Scotland; in fact, the rejection of Thatcher has served to underpin a sense of Scottish identity in the past three decades.

Pittock provides a view that argues that the period from the mid to late twentieth century saw a Scotland where policy centralisation was mixed with administrative devolution, which paralleled a decline in Scottish autonomy. What Scotland now accepts as being particularly Scottish policies are, according to Pittock, post-war policies developed centrally for British society. When policies changed in terms of content and focus after 1979, Scottish society did not recognise them and still has not accepted them. Yet this picture of economic and social change is wedded to the political arena. The initial period of centralising policies from the 1950s saw Scotland and England voting in similar fashion, despite the presence of a strong Scottish national identity. As changes occurred within the social realm, they also occurred within the political realm; voting patterns in Scotland diverged from those of England during the 1970s (Miller 1981), which would only become more pronounced in the 1980s and 1990s. Clear differences arose in political offerings, outcomes and opportunities in Scotland as nationalism became a constant political and electoral force.

NATIONALISM AND POLITICAL CHANGE IN SCOTLAND

As stated in the introduction to this chapter, Robert McIntyre was elected in 1945 as the first ever SNP MP. However, whatever hopes the party had of becoming successful in the immediate post-war period were soon dashed three short months later, as the party suffered dismal results in the 1945 General Election. The fact was that the SNP lacked the members and infrastructure, having suffered a split in 1942 from which it would take some time to recover. While it may have entertained thoughts of greater triumphs in the light of one by-election victory, the true success of the SNP was simply survival through to the 1960s (Hanham 1969) when it began to grow in strength. The 1945 by-election result was not at all indicative of true electoral or public support; as the election was fought under wartime conditions with no other challenger against Labour, the SNP clearly benefited. Nonetheless, the results of the 1945 General Election placed Conservatives third in Motherwell & Wishaw, behind the SNP. While this was not a harbinger of immediate Conservative decline in Scotland, that decline would set in two decades later, and the number of Conservative MPs in Scotland would continue to dwindle as the century progressed, ultimately reaching zero in 1997.

CONSERVATIVE DECLINE

Table 2.1 illustrates that the decline of the Conservative and Unionist Party is a clear trend in Scottish politics. This brand of distinctly Scottish Conservatism (McCrone 2001) had emerged in the early part of the twentieth century and the party would become the leading party of unionism in Scotland. The loss of support of the major vehicle for Union-ism in its original form correlates to the loss of support for traditional Unionism in Scotland today. Being so closely allied to the idea of Con-servatism has been a problem for Unionism in the post-1979 period and since the establishment of the Scottish Parliament, although recent election results may indicate that this trend has begun to reverse, albeit very slightly.

The Conservatives remained a significant force throughout the 1950s. At the 1955 election, they achieved two significant high points: first, they gained two more seats than Labour, and second, they gained vote share. The Conservatives remain the only party to have gained over 50 per cent of the Scottish electorate in the last sixty years, although the Labour Party gained 49.9 per cent in 1966. Thus, 1955 was the high tide of Scottish Conservatism and Unionism. The party seemed strong, in terms of both MPs and electoral support, and had weathered the change in political fortunes that had seen the rise of Labour and the fall of the Liberals. However, to place these results in perspective, we should note that the Liberal Party had regularly gained a significant proportion (often well over two-thirds) of the vote during the nineteenth century. Even when the Liberal decline began in the late 1800s, electoral results for the party still registered over 50 per cent support at every election until 1918.

Table 2.1 General Election results in Scotland: percentage of vote
(seats in brackets)

Election	Con	Lab	Lib Dem[a]	SNP	Total seats
1945[b]	41.1 (27)	49.4 (40)	5.0	1.2	71
1950	44.8 (32)	46.2 (37)	6.6 (2)	0.4	71
1951	48.6 (35)	47.9 (35)	2.7 (2)	0.3	71
1955	50.1 (36)	46.7 (34)	1.9 (1)	0.5	71
1959	47.2 (31)	46.7 (38)	4.1 (1)	0.8	71
1964	40.6 (24)	48.7 (43)	7.6 (4)	2.4	71
1966	37.7 (20)	49.9 (46)	6.8 (5)	5.0	71
1970	38.0 (23)	44.5 (44)	5.5 (3)	11.4 (1)	71
1974 (Feb)	32.93 (21)	36.63 (40)	7.94 (3)	21.93 (7)	71
1974 (Oct)	24.70 (16)	36.28 (41)	8.30 (3)	30.44 (11)	71
1979	31.41 (22)	41.54 (44)	8.99 (3)	17.29 (2)	71
1983	28.37 (21)	35.07 (41)	24.53 (8)	11.75 (2)	72
1987	24.02 (10)	42.39 (50)	19.21 (9)	14.04 (3)	72
1992	25.77 (11)	39.04 (49)	12.90 (9)	21.45 (3)	72
1997	17.53 (0)	45.63 (56)	12.99 (10)	21.94 (6)	72
2001[c]	15.58 (1)	43.27 (55)	16.34 (10)	20.06 (5)	72
2005[c]	15.8 (1)	38.9 (40)	22.6 (11)	17.7 (6)	59
2010	16.77 (1)	41.97 (41)	18.88 (11)	19.93 (6)	59

[a] This section includes the Liberals, the Alliance and the Liberal Democrats.
[b] Four other MPs were elected from Scotland – the last time any outwith the four parties listed have been elected.
[c] The Speaker was elected within Scotland (and previously sat as a Labour MP).

Nonetheless, the Conservative Unionists were significant in Scottish politics during the 1940s and 1950s, and would remain so for some years. In many respects, the party always faced an uphill battle. Even when the Conservatives gained a greater percentage of the vote than Labour, or a similar percentage, they gained fewer seats. In 1959, when the Conservatives led Labour by 0.5 per cent of the vote share, they trailed by seven seats. It would seem clear that a combination of the electoral system used at Westminster elections and the nature of the geographical distribution of party support in Scotland resulted in disadvantages. The Conservative vote share did not decline overnight. The lessening of electoral support that noticeably began in the 1960s was hastened in the early 1970s by a massive increase in SNP support, which became the beneficiary of anti-Tory voting (Leith and Steven 2010). Although the Conservatives rallied somewhat in 1979, this was not a return to strength, and the decline continued. This resulted in the party no longer having any MPs from Scotland in 1997. Although the party has continually returned one MP in recent elections (though not always from the same constituency), support at Westminster elections remains minimal and widely dispersed geographically.

It was (and is) the first-past-the-post voting system for Westminster that allowed the Conservatives to maintain a significant influence on Scotland, even while such influence was waning in Scotland. One of the initial impacts upon Conservative support was the resurgence of Liberalism in Scotland in areas in which the Tories had previously been successful. When the SNP emerged as an electoral force in the late 1960s and early 1970s, it also drew support from Conservative (and Labour) voters. Despite the additional support, the governance of Scotland was still often under Conservative control because of the continued strength of that party south of the border. It soon became clear that just because Scotland elected fewer Conservatives, Conservative policies would be applied to Scotland. This was the trend from 1979 onwards, which Pittock (2008) states has become part of the folklore of Scottish politics; Scotland voted Labour (and SNP and Liberal Democrat) but got Thatcherite policies instead. This idea of the 'democratic deficit' would fuel the continued decline of Conservative support and the rehabilitated idea of devolution for Scotland.

LIBERAL RESURGENCE

Alongside the obvious decline of the Conservatives, the resurgence of the Liberals/Liberal Democrats was equally obvious. From representative oblivion in 1945, they have emerged to a stable position in recent elections in terms of elected MPs. During the post-war period the party had been the third and fourth party in terms of electoral support, but since the late 1990s, it has been the second party in terms of Scottish MPs. The Liberals have benefited from the decline in Conservative support but have not unduly suffered from the rise of the SNP, although correlations between respective fortunes can be seen.

The major improvement began during the 1980s with the creation of the Social Democratic Party (SDP), which attracted Conservative support as well, although it was initially formed by four defectors from Labour. As Table 2.1 shows, the Liberal/SDP Alliance during the 1980s attracted votes from all the major parties, and in 1983 the SNP vote declined to the 1970 level. Likewise, the Conservative vote declined, and even Labour recorded a new post-war low of support in Scotland. While this level of support was unsustainable for the soon-to-be Liberal Democrats, they have maintained their level of MPs. In 2005 the Liberal Democrats achieved support at a level similar to that of the 1980s, which once again began to impact upon the support of the SNP and the Labour Party. Therefore, the party clearly benefits from 'protest' votes at some elections and thus is subject to fluctuations in such support depending on the fortunes of other parties. The results of the 2010 election strongly indicate such a trend, with the party being the only one of the four to see a decline in vote share. In addition, the formal coalition with the Conservative Party in the current British Government may bode ill for Liberal Democrats at the 2011 Holyrood elections, should they become identified with 'anti Scottish' Conservative policies.

LABOUR DOMINANCE AND DEVOLUTION REBORN

Of the main parties that are organised throughout Britain, it is Labour that has come to dominate Scottish politics in a manner reminiscent of the historical Liberals. Whereas Conservative support has declined and Liberal Democrat support has fluctuated of late, Labour still maintains a significant lead ahead of the other parties in terms of vote share and an even greater lead in terms of MPs elected. Even when the SNP emerged in the 1970s, Labour MPs still returned to Westminster in great numbers as the Scottish electorate split among other opponents. This was still the case with the revival of SNP fortunes during the 1990s and since the advent of legislative devolution, and Labour representation from Scotland remains at an all-time high. Despite SNP goals for the 2010 elections of up to twenty Nationalist MPs, Labour dominated the results again, electing forty-one MPs, with the SNP gaining six.

Labour delivered devolution to Scotland and, upon reflection of the stances that each party has had towards devolution, and in light of the General Election results of the past sixty years, only Labour would ever have been in a position to do so. Labour was dominant in 1945 and spent the 1950s vying with the Conservatives for electoral control in Scotland and the UK at large. This was the period of purely British politics and two-party hegemony; distinct aspects within Scottish voting patterns had not begun to emerge. As the main challengers, and then the party of opposition in Scotland, the Conservatives were unlikely to offer any form of support to a home rule idea. Likewise, Labour saw little electoral profit in supporting a cause that would bring no help in a dead-heat fight. This stance was confirmed in 1958 when the Scottish Council of Labour firmly rejected home rule as a policy. This decision altered the position the party had voiced (if not actively supported) for several decades. It also changed the nature of politics within Scotland. The Liberals remained committed to home rule but presented a poor shadow of former glory, and no major party now advocated any form of devolution. Such an action seemed perfectly rational. The SNP had fielded only two or three candidates at each General Election during the 1950s and had gained less than 1 per cent of the Scottish vote (Lynch 2002).

The 1960s were a period of great change for Scotland socially, economically and politically. Overall government public spending in Scotland increased, along with the claims about what such spending would bring (Gallagher 2009). Emigration was predicted to fall, as employment would rise to the influx of new industry that was to be encouraged though spending (Harvie and Jones 2000). Scotland was changing, and so was the idea of what defined Scotland. The initial results of such activity were positive for Labour. The 1966 elections saw the return of Labour Government with an increased and workable majority; thus, the efforts that had been made in Scotland would be continued with an eye to maintaining the primacy of Labour over the Conservative opposition in Scotland. Labour viewed the Scottish results with glee, only minimally falling short of an absolute majority of votes. The further decline in support for the Conservative and Unionist Party confirmed the Labour Party's view of itself as 'Scotland's Party'. Labour did not worry about nationalism, as the SNP remained a marginal force and seemingly presented no challenge.

Despite the positive growth, the post-1966 period was not as rosy for Labour as the economic picture began to change. Forecasts made prior to the election did not pan out as predicted, and growth, in terms of GDP and employment, was nowhere near the claims made, with more jobs lost than created (Gallagher 2009). The strength of the pound began to drop and a growing sense of unrest among the workforce added to the economic gloom, as did the appearance of several strike actions in Scotland. The popularity of the Labour Government declined as the economic outlook began to appear bleaker. In addition, there were several very unpopular policy stances within central government. Harvie and Jones (2000) identify three as being particularly unpopular with certain elements of the Scottish electorate. First was the pro-European stance of the Government. The UK had already attempted to negotiate entry into the EEC and doubtless would have been further down the road had it not been for the presence of De Gaulle as French President. The SNP was anti-European at this time and presented a clear choice when compared to the 'British' parties on the issue. The second and third unpopular policy choices were the related pro-Vietnam and pro-nuclear armament policies of the Wilson Government. The issue of military activity and war had been one of the first major policy issues that the SNP had taken a stance on during the Second World War, when the Nationalists challenged the authority of Westminster to draft Scots into the armed forces. While this had been an unpopular stance among the Scottish electorate (and a somewhat divisive issue for the fledging SNP), there remained a thread of this thought that stretched through to the much more modern SNP of the 1960s (and continues today). Once again, the main-stream 'British' parties were very similar on this stance, as they were on Europe. While in government, the Conservatives and Labour were not far apart on the idea of the UK retaining an independent nuclear arsenal; therefore, it would be the SNP who would benefit from the CND factor (Devine 2008). These policy stances serve as representative of both the changing nature of the debate and the rising unpopularity of Labour in the late 1960s. In addition, the fact remains that the Scottish electorate often had little in terms of choice between the Labour and the Conservative parties and had few other choices with which to engage. There can be little doubt that the Liberal Party had been the beneficiary of such a position, but there was another choice available – a clear Scottish choice.

The renowned by-election victory by Winnie Ewing at Hamilton should be considered within this overall picture. While her election did not result in a collapse in Labour support in Scotland (and the 2010 General Election results only confirm Labour dominance at British elections in Scotland), that support has fluctuated since the 1970s elections, having only just returned to the levels the party witnessed during the 1950s and 1960s. Clearly, Labour peaked at the 1966 election. There is evidence to suggest that even then the seemingly healthy state of Labour in terms of electoral share was simply serving to mask problems (Keating and Bleiman 1978). Scottish politics and the issue of Scottish nationalism would never be the same again after Hamilton, and all parties had to adapt to the presence of the SNP. 'Modern Scottish politics was born' (Mitchell 2009: 32), and by the mid 1970s it seemed that the SNP could 'break' the two-party system (Gallagher 2009).

The 1968 Labour Party Conference witnessed 'vehement attacks' (Keating and Bleiman 1978) on the concept of nationalism as a political force, but this was simply verbal hostility against a threat that had already materialised. The Hamilton by-election results, and the success of the SNP at local elections in 1968, resulted in significant rethinking on devolution. This occurred within the Labour Party as well as with the Conservatives, who also began to consider moves that addressed the 'national' issue within Scottish politics. This highlights the importance of the SNP as an early political force, whose strength was not in governing potential but in blackmail potential (Mitchell 2009). It was this perceived ability of the Nationalist party to challenge for votes and seats that brought devolution back onto the agenda in the late 1960s and early 1970s, as the capacity of the SNP to bite into Labour's Scottish heartlands grew (Lynch 2002).

The reactions of the Labour and Conservative leadership were fairly immediate. At the Scottish Conservative Annual Conference in 1968, Edward Heath proposed the creation of a Scottish Assembly to be elected to work alongside Westminster. The 1968 'Declaration of Perth' may well have argued against independence, but the overall reaction of Scottish Conservatives gathered at their annual conference was one of silence, probably brought about by surprise and disbelief (Mitchell 1996). While the Conservative Party entered the 1970 elections with a firm manifesto pledge for a very limited form of home rule, this and other commitments 'were gimmicks driven by short term electoral calculations' (Gallagher 2009). At the same time, Labour had also established a Royal Commission in December 1968 as a result of SNP victories and near misses in by-elections (Harvie 1998) that would investigate the workings of the British Constitution. Thus, Labour had not committed itself to any form of devolution but could claim that it simply awaited the report of the Royal (Kilbrandon) Commission, which would spend 'years taking minutes'. Such actions were undertaken for one simple reason; by the end of the 1960s, nationalism was back on the agenda as a result of the electoral support shown for the SNP.

The Rise of the SNP and Devolution Reconsidered

The electoral breakthrough the SNP made in the late 1960s may, by contemporary consideration, appear logical, yet there was little reason to expect such an explosive re-ordering of the political landscape and the political agenda in both Scotland and the UK. The Hamilton by-election win was central in that it moved the SNP firmly into the public spotlight, and Winnie Ewing's media exposure over the next three years kept it there. Brand (1978) argues that it was this event that marked the arrival of the SNP for the majority of the Scottish electorate. While nationalism had long been an aspect of the political landscape in Scotland, it had remained peripheral and had never had serious governmental consideration during any part of the mid twentieth century. This was not going to be the case during the 1970s and onwards, when the electoral success of the SNP would cause devolution to become an active consideration of all political parties.

The SNP had developed a strong internal core during the late 1950s and early 1960s and had brought together a series of dedicated individuals who were politically astute as well as dedicated to the cause of independence (Lynch 2002). Perhaps for the first time, the SNP became a political party in more than name as the new wave in the party brought fresh ideas and activity. They represented a set of new activists who would help build the SNP up over the next three decades from a peripheral to a mainstream political organisation (Mitchell 2009). Nonetheless, the events of 1967 onwards must be considered within the wider context, and the electoral shifts must be considered as part of a greater trend than simply a sudden shift towards more nationalistic voting behaviour. In the 1970 General Election, the SNP lost Hamilton but gained the Western Isles from Labour. The SNP continued to garner support and created a true furore in the 1974 elections, with first seven and then eleven MPs, which pushed the Conservatives into third place in terms of vote share and coming second in many Labour constituencies. These results ensured that the idea of Scottish independence was firmly on the political agenda, and the concept of Scottish national identity as an organising political principle was no longer marginal.

The immediate result of the continued presence of the SNP was reconsideration by Labour on devolution. In 1973, the Scottish Council of the Labour Party pre-empted the Kilbrandon Report by firmly rejecting the idea of an assembly, but this decision was overturned by a special party conference in Glasgow in 1973. SNP success in 1974 resulted in the Labour Government introducing a Scotland and Wales Bill in February 1977, which contained serious issues for both supporters and detractors of home rule. Twenty-two Labour MPs (two Scots among them) assisted in defeating the Bill, but the Government introduced another in November 1977, or rather two separate Bills, which made it through Parliament by conceding a referendum. However, the Cunningham Amendment, which would require 40 per cent of the Scottish electorate to support the referendum, was attached – against government wishes.

The idea that these actions would have taken place had the SNP not gained such a level of electoral support is not conceivable, but the results were not positive for the Nationalist party. The 1979 referendum saw 51.6 per cent vote YES for creating a Scottish Assembly; however, because this represented only 32.9 per cent of the registered electorate it did not meet the requirements of the Cunningham Amendment. The Scotland Act was repealed in March 1979. Parts of rural southern and northern Scotland had provided no majorities, and the SNP tabled a motion of no confidence in the Government, which passed by one vote (Devine 2008). In a twist of political irony, the SNP was reduced to only two MPs in the ensuing General Election and the party entered a period of decline and internal disputes over the next few years.

Whatever the problems of the SNP, the wider nationalism movement continued to express support for some form of Scottish devolution. The Campaign for a Scottish Assembly (CSA) was set up in March 1980 as a direct result of the 1979 referendum (Mitchell 1996). This was a cross-party organisation, seeking to gain input from all sections of Scottish society. Although the CSA was never a major group in terms of numbers, it had a number of affiliated organisations and sought support from across the socio-political spectrum, although much activity was directed at the Labour Party. There was little success among Conservatives, with any representation being very much a fringe element, especially beyond local government level. The major problem was avoiding identification with one party or another. Initial strong SNP activity caused issues with Labour, who were suspicious of the aims of the CSA, and later the same problem was to exist in reverse, with the SNP suspicious of heavy Labour involvement. There was public support for the organisation, with an opinion poll in 1984 interpreted by the media as indicative of continued support within the public for devolution (Mitchell 1996).

The idea of a constitutional convention became moot within the CSA on a number of occasions, but after the 1987 election, the CSA formed a committee charged with the development of plans for a constitutional convention.[4] This committee reported back on 6 July 1988 with a document entitled 'A Claim of Right for Scotland'. The title was chosen (like the National Covenant of the 1950s) to provide a sense of historical continuity through other documents similarly titled in 1689 and 1842; supporters also claimed the tradition reached back to other documents such as the Declaration of Arbroath in 1320 (Edwards 1989).

In March 1989, fifty-eight Labour and Liberal Democrat MPs signed a

---

[4] The SNP had come round to the idea of a convention at its 1984 national conference.

Covenant and the Scottish Constitutional Convention was established (Gallagher 2009). Various bodies participated in the Convention, including Labour, the Liberal Democrats, the Scottish Greens, the Scottish Trades Union Congress and other civic bodies; it was the strong involvement of Labour (and arguably the domination of the convention by the Labour Party) that led to the withdrawal of the SNP. Mitchell (1996) argues that the SNP could not accept being a minority within the organisation, but it is also dismissed as an 'inept' manoeuvre (Gallagher 2009). The Conservative Government had not accepted the Claim of Right and was aggressively unwelcoming toward the convention, going so far as to challenge local authority involvement. The SNP became very anti-convention and had little to do with the subsequent events. Nevertheless, there can be little doubt that the Convention was extremely influential in informing the debate about devolution, and the publication of *Scotland's Parliament, Scotland's Right* in 1995 set forth a document that would serve as a basis for the structure of the future Scottish Parliament.

THE 1997 REFERENDUM

The massive Labour vote at the 1997 General Election ensured a devolution referendum in Scotland, which the party had committed to in 1995. A two-part plebiscite, one focusing on the establishment of a parliament, the other seeking limited tax authority for that parliament, was proposed. The 1997 referendum campaign was in strong contrast to that of the 1970 referendum (McGarvey and Cairney 2008). All the major parties, excepting the Conservatives, supported the idea and worked together to gain a majority for the YES/YES vote. In September 1997, 74.3 per cent of those voting on the first question agreed and 63.3 per cent voting on the second question agreed. In 1998, the Scotland Act was passed by Westminster. It has been argued that Scottish voters supported the idea of the Parliament because of their wish to 'improve welfare in the widest sense of the term' (McCrone 2001: 124), not necessarily as a result of a strong focus on being Scottish. Such arguments contend that people thought those supportive political parties could deliver on this promise, thus the electorate supported them when voting for that Parliament.

DEVOLUTION DELIVERED: VOTING IN SCOTLAND SINCE 1999

The establishment of the Scottish Parliament in 1999 marked the culmination of decades of effort by a myriad of groups seeking a variety of political solutions, including home rule, devolution and independence for Scotland.

Mitchell (1996) has argued that there are four routes to self-government, all of which can be found in the case of Scotland. These include home rule pressure groups, constitutional conventions, petitions and referenda, and parties that campaign for constitutional change. While all of these have been employed at various times by the national movement in Scotland, it was ultimately a combination of them, operating during the 1980s and 1990s, that brought the Scottish Parliament into being. With the inception of the Parliament, Scottish nationalism surged, as the SNP firmly entered the political mainstream and became a truly parliamentary party, thereby gaining the potential to govern (Mitchell 2009).

Table 2.2 Scottish Parliament election results: percentage of vote (seats in brackets); smaller parties and independents not included

Election	Con	Lab	Lib Dem	SNP	Green	SSP
1999 (Con)	15.56 (0)	38.81 (53)	14.15 (12)	28.74 (7)	–	1.01 (0)
1999 (List)	15.35 (18)	33.64 (3)	12.43 (5)	27.26 (28)	3.59 (1)	1.99 (1)
2003 (Con)	16.53 (3)	34.89 (46)	15.13 (13)	23.77 (9)	–	6.22 (0)
2003 (List)	15.50 (15)	29.30 (4)	11.78 (4)	20.86 (18)	6.68 (7)	6.90 (6)
2007 (Con)	16.60 (4)	32.15 (37)	16.17 (11)	32.93 (21)	0.15 (0)	N/A
2007 (List)	13.91 (13)	29.16 (9)	11.30 (5)	31.02 (26)	4.04 (2)	N/A

What is clear from the Scottish Parliament election results is that the patterns reflect similarities and differences with British elections. The Conservatives and Liberal Democrats received support that was broadly in keeping with their results from recent General Elections. Yet, the Liberal Democrats gained a significant number of constituency MSPs, thus reducing their proportional support, while the Conservatives initially owed all of their MSPs, and the majority since, to an electoral system they strongly opposed. Conservative support has remained steady, only fluctuating within a 1 per cent range, except in 2007. Similarly, support for the Liberal Democrats has been limited. The Liberal Democrats were not able to capitalise on their 2005 General Election performance in either 2003 or 2007, which indicates a difference in voter behaviour when it comes to different institutions. While they served as the minority partner in coalition from 1999 to 2003 and from 2003 to 2007, this does not seem to have strongly impacted upon their support.

Most importantly, Labour has been less successful in Scottish elections than in British elections in Scotland. It received leading vote shares in 1999 and 2003, formed the majority partner in governmental coalitions after both and continues to dominate the constituency aspect of Scottish elections. However, its vote share in the constituency result has declined at every election, and in 2007 it became the second party in terms of MSPs, with the SNP beating it by one and also overtaking it in terms of vote share gained. In 2007 the SNP managed to reverse a trend whereby the 1999 results is a high point, with 2003 a significant disappointment. The Nationalist party now constitutes a minority government in the Scottish Parliament, with 47 MSPs out of a total of 129, and has realised its governing potential, seven decades after being established. This is the key characteristic of the Scottish parliamentary system. The results of the 1970 and 1974 elections provided the SNP with a limited institutional and establishment base from which to operate and build upon; the Scottish Parliament has provided a much more effective and focused means to do so. The location of the Parliament, in Scotland, and the central role that it plays in day-to-day Scottish society has served the profile of the SNP in a manner that Westminster could never do. Ultimately, the creation of a parliament in Scotland was one further step in enhancing the national identity aspect of Scottish politics. The formation of the first SNP Scottish Government has additionally enhanced the emphasis on Scottish nationalism and independence.

CONCLUSIONS

National identity has long been a component of the Scottish people, and nationalism has long been a part of Scottish politics, but it is only within the last forty or so years that both have entered the ongoing political arena and only in the last decade that they have occupied centre stage on a regular basis. From being represented by a peripheral, often seemingly ephemeral, movement, by a party that struggled to produce any meaningful level of candidates, political nationalism is now a constant. Only thirty years ago, the idea of a Scottish legislative body had been rejected by Westminster, and the SNP had been reduced to a rump presence in that Parliament. Although the nationalist movement in Scotland responded with the creation of a wide-ranging socio-political body, it too initially operated in a very limited and publicly disregarded fashion.

When the nationalist movement regained the public fore with the design for a Scottish parliament, it was a movement that included individuals from a number of parties and organisations, but not from the SNP. The nationalist movement came together and created the blueprints for the Scottish Parliament and laid the firm groundwork for a referendum in

Scotland. The movement had drawn from a wide spectrum that included the foremost party of Scottish politics, Labour; it ultimately needed the support of this dominant party in ensuring that a referendum took place. This reflects once again the simple fact that nationalism is not, and has never been, the sole preserve of one political organisation or party in Scotland; rather, a strong sense of national identity permeates the country's entire political system. Furthermore, this national identity has been an enduring constant in Scottish society, but often quiescent within Scottish politics. This is no longer the case. It is now clear that the prevalent political idea in Scotland is that Scotland is a nation with a distinct identity, operating in a distinct fashion, requiring distinct political answers.

The following chapter will begin to illustrate how the nationalist–unionist issue has changed over the last forty years in Scottish politics, with the later chapters providing a comparative between elite, political employment of national identity and wider public opinion.

3

The Changing Sense of Scotland: the Political Employment of National Identity

We now turn to a consideration of the political focus on national identity and nationalism in Scottish manifestos issued for British General Elections from the 1970s onwards. We specifically employ a quantitative framework, allowing the measurement of political and nationalist positioning of the four major parties on two spectrums, measuring the past forty years. In addition, a consideration of specific aspects employing appeals to a sense of national identity (Scottishness or Britishness) is undertaken. As political documents the manifestos seek to project a stance on the nationalist–unionist debate – a stance that allows the parties to create a sense of 'them' and 'us'. Crucially, this sense of identity is both political and national. Parties are (obviously) seeking votes for the election in question, but at the same time the projection of national identity within the manifestos also has an influence on the overall nature of Scottishness. As parties look to create an ideological, political platform in Scotland, this platform also impacts, and is impacted upon by, the sense of national identity in Scotland.

SCOTLAND APART

The political and electoral activity that takes place within Scotland as well as the Scottish party system display significant differences from the wider British system of which it is a part. These differences are evident today in areas such as electoral results and opportunities for mainstream (and lesser) political parties. There is a much wider spectrum of political parties operating in Scotland at an elected level, or with the opportunity to gain representation at that level. However, the vast majority of Scottish MPs and MSPs and councillors are elected from the four main parties, and it is these parties that we focus on. The establishment of the Scottish Parliament in 1999 created a system that existed both within and separately from the greater UK. For the first time in the history of the UK decisions being made by an elected legislature actually within Scotland, chosen by an electorate being limited to Scottish residents, became a reality. Today few argue that a truly particular and separate (albeit still subordinate) Scottish political system does not exist.

The identification and recognition of a Scottish political system did not come about with legislative devolution. A distinct political system has long existed, and different institutions and differing political and electoral behaviour within Scotland have been a political reality for decades. Kellas (1973; 1984) was among the first to discuss and argue for the recognition of a discrete political system in Scotland, although he appreciated that one could not always provide an unambiguous understanding between the British and Scottish aspects. The separate civil and legal institutions that Scotland possessed created the basis for such a system. In addition, the political parties themselves were recognised as being recognisably different from their southern brethren (Brown et al. 1996). Thus Scotland operated as part of the mainstream politics of Westminster and the UK, but with specific characteristics of its own. There were detractors from this position (Mitchell 2003), and the awareness of a semi-detached Scottish system did not lead to the UK being recognised as a non-unitary state. Although the UK was a 'union-state' (Rokkan and Urwin 1983) the popular political conception of Britain as nothing less than a unitary state would not become openly challenged until the dawn of legislative devolution.

Because of the interpretation of the UK as a unitary state, the study of Scotland and Scottish politics was not a primary academic pursuit for much of the twentieth century, despite the fact that Scotland retained several institutional and political singularities that evidently set it apart. Examinations of Scotland did illustrate the continued existence of a particular civil society that aided in the maintenance and growth of a separate national identity (Paterson 1994; Keating 2001), which was conceived of as civic in form. While the Scottish case was recognised as illustrating that 'the theory of British political homogeneity has been proved to be defective' (Budge and Urwin 1966: 132) the challenges wrought by this separate identity were thought 'outside the field of party competition' (Budge and Urwin 1966: 138). While the argument focused on the distinct institutional aspects of Scotland rather than the competition among political parties, one important party political caveat was noted: 'the widespread existence of Scottish loyalties provides support for the activities of the Home Rule movement but also – and to date more important – that it buttresses the autonomy of the Scottish sections of the two major parties' (Budge and Urwin 1966: 133). The Scottish sectors of the major political parties, even without the presence of an electorally challenging Nationalist party, did operate a certain amount of autonomy. This varied between parties but existed as part of the wider system. Devolution has only emphasised this autonomy among Labour and the Conservatives, bringing them closer in form to the federalised Liberal Democrats and the solely Scottish SNP.

By downplaying the significance of national identity within the party system Budge and Urwin missed recognising the full impact a Nationalist party could have on the autonomy of the Scottish wings of parties. Their caveat did serve to highlight the impending, unexpected impact upon the political system within Scotland that the electoral growth of the independence-seeking SNP and the home rule-supporting Liberal Party would have when the mid 1960s saw the stirrings of support for the SNP and the Liberals. The changes that the next few decades brought only serve to increase the need to understand the nature of national identity in Scotland from a political perspective. Time and increasing electoral support for these 'third' parties also underwrote the importance to the major two parties of the British electorate system of considering and addressing Scotland as a particular entity.

Today British parties must take into account a Scottish dimension when formulating policy. Three of the major political parties that operate within both the British and Scottish contexts thus need to address the issue of a Scottish identity and context. The SNP has the distinct advantage of not presenting candidates for election within other areas of the UK. The other three parties have to be both British and Scottish at the same time, balancing their activities, actions and policies with the UK dimension in mind. There are times when this policy balancing act is more than just difficult; it can become a situation where any avenue would leave a party open to attack by the other political parties and organisations operating in the Scottish or British political arena. For example, if in government, both Labour and the Conservatives must seek to balance future defence needs with keeping the remaining Clyde shipbuilding interests open. To cut orders for future Royal Navy vessels because of budgetary constraints may play well to Conservative supporters in England, but leaves the party open to attacks of being 'anti-Scottish'. Likewise Labour must ensure it does not alienate Scottish supporters in a geographic region where the SNP has successfully challenged for parliamentary seats. All major political parties operating in Scotland must both project and reflect a sense of national identity that sections of the electorate can recognise and be comfortable with as they provide the link with civil society, institutions and the wider public (Heywood 2002).

Parties in any democratic political system face a challenge as they seek to expand their support base. They must construct a platform and an image that is appealing to as wide a group of voters as possible. They must maintain a recognisable party ideology (which links them to that core group of voters) while not significantly compromising key aspects of that ideology. This general picture of party activity becomes even more complicated when taking place in a sub-state, national dimension such as Scotland. The case of Scotland, a nation subsumed within the larger UK state, to which the national area elects a minority number of legislators, is a prime example of an area where national identity, party politics and nationalism combine. Only limited work has been undertaken to consider how political parties operating both within Scotland and the wider UK have employed a sense of national identity within their core documents, although the existence of nationalist activity and a strong national identity in Scotland creates an opportunity to understand how the political parties deal with these facts of political life.

Elites regularly employ the relationship between nationalism and history in their attempts to create, maintain and legitimise the nation and a sense of nationhood (A. D. Smith 2003). Modernists emphasise how elites legitimise nationalist ideas by employing the past as a tool in the present (Breuilly 1996; Calhoun 1997), while ethno-symbolists such as Anthony D. Smith (1986, 2003) show the importance of the historical myths and symbols drawn from the *ethnie*, the durable, ethnic communities of history. Employing the past of golden ages and mythical heroes to more recent, and perhaps mundane, political events regularly takes place. As Coakley makes quite clear: 'The capacity of elites to shape political outcomes by influencing the way in which the past is perceived and interpreted is a well known characteristic of public life' (2004: 531), and national history is an important tool for political elites in their quest to create the national future. This is especially important in Scotland where national identity is a widespread phenomenon within the social and political arena. No one party can claim sole ownership of that identity (although some may argue they can). Indeed, the relationship between national identity, party support and constitutional preference is extremely complex (Bond 2000). National political elites employ nationalist symbols and myths to support their political programme, but even those parties that do not seek to alter the fundamental political relationship between Scotland and the rest of the UK articulate nationalist imagery as part of their contribution to the political debate. While not nationalist in the traditional sense of seeking a nation and state with congruent borders, the Conservatives are still engaged in the nationalist debate of Scotland.

Speeches and other commentary of political leaders abound with symbolic statements and national myths, as do the central policy planks of the parties within Scotland. The manifestos issued within Scotland during the period of rising support for the SNP provide an opportunity to examine how the major parties have engaged with the national focus and nationalist dimensions of Scottish politics.

CONSIDERING MANIFESTOS

The Comparative Manifesto Project (CMP) has produced an extraordinary depth and range of research in the study of party platforms (see, for example, Budge et al. 2001; Budge et al. 1987; Budge and Farlie 1983; Klingemann et al. 2006). While the examination of 'British' manifestos has been a significant focus of research, analysis of their separate Scottish counterparts has not previously been undertaken using the methodology employed by the CMP. Nonetheless, such research provides areas for analysis in relation not only to national identity and nationalism, but also to the overall position of parties within the Scottish political system. The scheme itself translates the text of a manifesto into a percentage-based measurement tool. It allows for the individual coding of statements within the documents, coding each sentence, or quasi-sentence, where two or more distinct ideas are contained within one full sentence, into specific policy areas. The relative importance given to specific policy areas can then be considered by measuring the individual codes against the total statements within the document. These coded statements are further grouped into seven specific policy areas, such as 'Freedom and Democracy', 'Economy', Welfare and Quality of Life' and 'Fabric of Society'.[1]

The original CMP coding scheme did not prioritise, or perhaps consider, the need to measure a sub-state political system, and modification in order to undertake such an analysis was required, although significant work to adapt the scheme has subsequently taken place (see Klingemann et al. 2006). From the perspective of the Scottish political debates on nationalism, national identity and politics, there is significant crossover between the areas of 'Freedom and Democracy' and 'The Political System', both considered as distinct policy areas by the CMP, as statements and policy positions within Scottish manifestos draw upon both areas for supporting devolution and independence as policies. Significant aspects of the discussion on devolution have tended to focus on the democratic issues involved, with other arguments focused on the constitutional issues, or even the related, and often minor, issue of the EU.

[1] A fuller explanation and description of the methodological coding scheme is provided in the Appendix.

Along similar lines, the original CMP scheme problematically equated patriotism with nationalism; a position not suitable for the study of a political system contained within a recognised national area yet subsumed within a larger state. Patriotic appeals, within the Scottish manifestos of Labour or the Conservatives (the Liberal Democrats tend to avoid such appeals) are directed towards the idea of Britishness and Britain, but this is not the case for nationalism. Nationalist appeals, be they culturally, historically or politically motivated, are firmly and undeniably Scottish, with the Scottish nation as the base unit. Opposition to the existing state structure is the driving force behind the SNP, and the conflation of nation and state was so apparent within the original CMP system that changes were required for the analysis to be conceptually and methodologically sound. Linked issues, such as the original system requiring the inclusion of Gaelic language policy under a multicultural code, pointed to the additional need for adaptation of the scheme. Therefore, additional categories were created to allow for specific references to the Union and the policy of devolution, and to allow for the analysis of nationalist sentiments within the manifestos of all the parties. This provided a total of sixty-three discrete categories, across seven domains, as listed in the Appendix.

While only a small portion of the public read the actual manifestos (Brack 2000) they are widely mediated to the public throughout the election campaign. Manifesto launches in Scotland today are media events in themselves, with pictures of the party leaders proudly displaying the manifesto being shown on the evening news and in newspapers. These documents are the statement of policies and programmes for the future – the central feature of any political party at that election. The winning party within a British election will claim their victory as a mandate by which they may enact the policies contained within the manifesto itself. Even when the winning party does not hold a majority of Scottish seats, that party will still govern the entire UK, as the 2010 General Election illustrates.

In short, manifestos 'are the best-known documents produced by the British political parties' (Cooke 2000: 1); they are written with 'immense care' and a focus on them allows for an examination of each party across both time and space (Kavanagh 2000). Therefore, we argue that examination of the political formation and employment of Scottish national identity, and how that identity interacts within and impacts on Scottish politics, can be informed by an analysis of the Scottish version of British political manifestos, which are national political platforms and have been prior to the establishment of the national, devolved legislature in 1999.

Modern manifestos are produced for every major election (Budge et al. 2001; Rosenbaum 1997) but this was not the case for much of the twentieth century in Scotland. Their initial employment was sporadic, with the Conservative and Labour parties issuing some separate manifestos for Scotland during the 1950s. It was not until the 1970s that all the major 'British' parties began to regularly produce separate and distinct Scottish manifestos. Obviously the SNP has been issuing manifestos with a purely Scottish focus for a much longer period, and for many years its had been the only decisively Scottish manifesto in that it was the only one exclusively aimed at the Scottish electorate alone. But the increasing strength of the SNP and its elected presence at Westminster changed that dynamic. Since the early 1970s, all the major political parties have produced distinct Scottish manifestos at all British General Elections. We now undertake an analysis of the General Election manifestos issued for Scotland from 1970 to 2010, with a specific assessment of how parties have engaged with and employed national identity in their core party documents, beginning with the study of areas of policy emphasis.

THE POLITICAL DIFFERENCE

Our analysis focuses on specific policies and the wider seven specific categories, or domains, within which, as discussed above, individual policies are grouped. These specific domains are:

1: External Relations
2: Freedom and Democracy
3: Political System
4: Economy
5: Welfare and Quality of Life
6: Fabric of Society
7: Social Groups

All the parties have maintained, throughout most of the last forty years, a focus on two general areas within the domains entitled Economy and Welfare and Quality of Life. It is quite rare for parties to give other areas greater emphasis than either of these two broad policy domains, although the exception to this was generally the Conservatives who often eclipsed their consideration of Welfare and Quality of Life with a focus on the Political System.

The area that often received less attention from the major political parties is policies concerning the Fabric of Society, such as social harmony or law and order. Apart from the SNP in 1983 this area rarely saw any party dedicate more than 10 per cent of its comments to that area. Overall this domain was one of the least-considered areas within the manifestos during the 1970s and 1980s. This pattern began to change during the 1990s as criminal policy emerged as an area of strong focus for most of the parties. In 1997 Labour devoted 11.26 per cent of its manifesto towards discussion on the Fabric of Society, most of it centring on the discussion of law and order issues; it was surpassed by both the SNP with 13.6 per cent and the Conservatives with 13.73 per cent. This pattern was generally repeated in the 2001 British General Election, when Labour spent 11.18 per cent of its manifesto on policies in this area and the SNP 12.15 per cent; the Conservatives, however, increased their focus on such policies, with 16.06 per cent of their manifesto dedicated to the Fabric of Society. While this area was a priority for these parties, the Liberal Democrat emphasis was only just under 10 per cent of the party's 1997 manifesto, dropping significantly in 2001 to 2.01 per cent and moving it even further out of the prevailing political focus. While the Fabric of Society remained an area of priority for Labour and the Conservatives in 2005, both the SNP and the Liberal Democrats focused their efforts on policy issues such as Freedom and Democracy. By 2010, the SNP, with 16.18 per cent, had four times more emphasis in this policy arena, mainly due to its discussion of independence, than either Labour or the Conservatives, at 5.18 per cent and 4.88 per cent respectively, and still greater than that of the Liberal Democrats, who dedicated 11.3 per cent of their manifesto to such policies.

We can, therefore, measure differences among the parties, both at specific elections and across time. Such differences as we have discussed here have implications for both political support and issues of national identity. At a General Election, each party will be playing to its base strength, attempting to focus the political debate in those areas it sees as significant for its potential supporters and/or for that specific election. This is the main reason that the SNP and the Liberal Democrats have often spent more time discussing issues of Freedom and Democracy than the two main parties. These two parties have argued for constitutional and political changes in Scotland, and the wider UK; although at times they have been surpassed in that policy area by other parties. In 1997 the Conservative manifesto dedicated 16.06 per cent to Freedom and Democracy, representing a much greater emphasis on this area than the party had ever given before (or has done since). Unlike the Liberal Democrat rhetoric and proposed policies, with a similar 13.07 per cent manifesto highlighting of these issues, the Conservative emphasis was on the defence of the status quo, and an attack on devolution as a dismantling of the Union. Labour, the party that would shortly deliver on devolution as a policy, had the lowest emphasis at this time, with only 9.68 per cent of its manifesto focused on such issues, making it its second smallest domain for discussion at the time.

The importance given to specific policies and domains within the documents may change as a result of factors to which the parties are responding rather than driving. Each election platform will be manufactured around specific issues, and others will arise during the campaign, that may affect the tone of the election and be taken into consideration during the formation and production of the next manifestos. As we discussed above, the 1997 and 2001 manifestos saw both Labour and the Conservatives paying significant attention to the subjects of anti-social behaviour and crime, yet the Liberal Democrats and the SNP chose not to do so, a pattern also repeated in 2010. Just over 1 per cent of the Liberal Democrat manifesto in 1997 specifically discussed the issue of crime, although it was a considerable part of election rhetoric for the other parties. So the changes and differences that exist over time are representative not only of the shifting preferences of the party involved but also of other demands within the political and social system.

While parties generally, as they must, give attention to a broad range of ideas and policies within their manifestos, they also differ markedly in relation to what they believe significant. The various parties seek to establish a more dominant position in the Scottish political system and in doing so they provide not only a party political ideology, but also a classic nationalistic sense of 'us' and 'them'. This 'us' differentiates the in-group from the 'them' of the out-group, their political opponents. Within the Scottish system a nationalist cleavage exists apart from the left–right ideological one, and thus the sense of another 'us' and 'them' must also be given, these latter groups providing boundaries for the nation beyond the political left or right. For any nation to exist and be considered separate there must be a sense of belonging to the nation. This means that out-groups will be created – individuals or other groups who do not belong to the nation – and parties will seek to portray their political opponents as not operating in the national interest. We shall now specifically investigate how the parties differentiated themselves from their opponents, not just in terms of a focus on specific policies or general policy areas, but on ideologically based grounds, before undertaking a similar consideration of national identity.

PARTY POLITICAL DIFFERENCES – THE LEFT–RIGHT DIVIDE IN SCOTLAND

We can measure and allow for how parties score on an ideological left-to-right political scale. The scale is created by adding percentage scores within categories, which are grouped as either left or right respectively, and then subtracting the sum of the left from that of the right. This measurement provides 'a score for each party-in-an-election based on its official programme, indicating where it was in Left-Right terms' (Klingemann et al. 2006: 5). While this specific approach has been challenged (McLean 2006; Pelizzo 2003; Dinas and Gemenis 2010), long-term analysis and employment indicates good measurement validity and empirical applicability (Klingemann et al. 2006). For greater specifics of the methodological approach, see Laver and Budge (1992).

As employed here, this scale indicates how the parties have positioned themselves ideologically within the Scottish, not British, political system. This distinction that we emphasise is that the party positions discussed are particular to Scotland and indicate the movement of parties against each other and in relation to one another within the Scottish political system. This system must be taken as a distinct polity due to the presence of political nationalism within Scotland. There are other political parties that advocate independence for Scotland (the Scottish Greens or the Scottish Socialists, for instance) but the SNP remains the only mainstream party elected to Westminster that promotes this policy. At the same time, there is the recognition of the Scottish electorate as being slightly more politically to the left than the English electorate (Bennie et al. 1997). Therefore, it could be argued that any party seeking to establish itself as an effective political force in favour of nationalism in Scotland would have to position itself to the left of the political spectrum to make a significant electoral impact. For example, McCrone (2001) has referred to this in relation to the Conservatives finding themselves since the late 1990s in an 'ideological cul-de-sac' in Scottish politics.

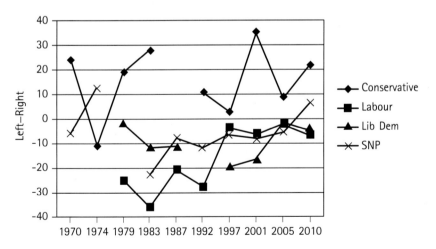

Figure 3.1 Left–Right spectrum: Scotland 1970–2010

Positioning on the left–right political scale indicates significant changes within the Scottish political arena over the last forty years. Overall, while it has been claimed that the SNP is 'difficult to pin down on the ideological spectrum' (McGarvey and Cairney 2008: 49), Figure 3.1 indicates that there has been limited movement for the party across the political spectrum since 1970. The claim often made that the SNP in the early to mid 1970s were 'Tories' with a specifically Scottish focus ('Tartan Tories') is plausible given the data. But specific analysis of the results indicates that the slight left-wing position of the SNP in 1970 was due to the focus within its manifesto on Freedom and Democracy issues, and a significantly reduced focus in this area in 1974 was one of the factors that contributed to its crossing into the right wing of the political spectrum. The Tartan Tories label applied in the 1970s does indeed have some validity in terms of the focus of the party's policies during that period. However, during the 1980s the SNP shifted to the left of the political centre, a move that could be attributed to the party looking to challenge Labour in Scotland (McEwen 2002). In fact, during the early elections of the twentieth century the SNP was the only party to state openly its position in Scottish politics: a left-of-centre party. Yet in 2010, the SNP again shifted to the right of the political spectrum, a move due to several factors. In terms of the manifesto data, in 2010 the SNP took a strong pro-business focus within its policies, with almost one-fifth of the manifesto dedicated to such discussion, and this provides a significant aspect of the shift to the right in policy terms. Recently, the SNP has sought to emphasis its pro-business credentials and support economic development in Scotland. Furthermore, this move has occurred while the SNP is the governing party in Scotland and may reflect the realities of a party seeking to govern, rather than a party committed to a particular ideological position (Leith and Steven 2010). In addition, tonal differences between SNP manifestos for Westminster elections and those for Holyrood elections are evident, and so the party may be positioning itself differently with different elections in mind.

Taken as an overall view, these policy shifts may well reflect the general trend of British politics in recent years, with a general movement of several parties towards the centre-right. The British Labour Party moved to the right of the political spectrum during the 1990s (Bara and Budge 2001) as it fought to gain electoral support and win seats beyond its traditional geographic and electoral areas of support. As the SNP also aims to increase its electoral returns at General Elections, it may well engage with areas of support that it has not done so since the early 1970s, when significant gains in traditional Conservative seats were made. Finally, it must be remembered that that the SNP is a Nationalist party and while it has long rested on the centre-left of the political spectrum, its shift to the right serves to illustrate the traditional cleave of nationalism as a political ideology, where the concepts of right wing and left wing have less efficacy than the idea of national independence.

Unsurprisingly, the Conservatives have occupied the right of the political spectrum within Scotland for the majority of the period in question, with the exception of 1974. Their position at this time was moderately left of centre. Our analysis indicates that this curious exception was mainly due to a focus within that manifesto on Welfare and Quality of Life issues. With 23.07 per cent of their Scottish manifesto dedicated to this general area, the Conservatives had more than doubled their 1970 emphasis on these policies. Whilst not singular in itself, as they would approach this figure again in 1992, when allied to the absence of the traditional Tory focus on law and order and international issues, the party provided a platform more to the left than it ever has since. There is little reason to doubt the accuracy of the data interpretation, or the placement of the Conservatives due to that data. The October 1974 elections pitted the SNP against the Scottish Conservatives and Unionist Party, and, aware of this challenge, the Conservatives may have modified their focus, and their language. By the next election the Scottish Conservatives had regained their traditional locale and have remained on and to the right of the other parties since.

Overall, distinct patterns emerge from this analysis of the Scottish left–right political spectrum. One is that the SNP and the Labour Party have similar trajectory patterns up to 2010. Labour's movement was more greatly pronounced during the 1990s; the party passed the SNP from the left during the late 1990s and very early part of the twenty-first century, becoming more consistently centrist. Nonetheless both parties have moved, from more pronounced left-wing positions in 1979 towards more centrist positions today. Comparatively the Labour Party has remained on the left of the Scottish political spectrum, although this has not been the case in the UK. As Bara and Budge pointed out, 'by 1997 Labour moved rightwards and "leapfrogged" over [the Liberal Democrats] for only the second time in the post-war period, in relative terms, *Labour became the most centrist party*' (2001: 594 original emphasis). This situation was mirrored in Scotland, when the Liberals moved to the left in 1997 and Labour made a significant shift to the centre. However, in Scotland, Labour's left–right score in 1997 was still on the left of the political spectrum, at –3.65, while the 'British' Labour Party was on the right at 8.03 (Bara and Budge 2001). 'Scottish' Labour may have positioned itself to the right of the SNP and the Liberal Democrats, but it remained significantly to the left in comparison to the British Labour stance and in 2010 became, in a limited fashion, the most left-wing Scottish party again.

A different result occurs with a direct comparison of Scottish and British manifesto data for the Liberal Democrats' and Conservatives' scores. In Scotland the Conservative Party had begun to swing to the right from its 1992 position. In 1997 the Scottish manifesto achieved a left–right score of 21.67. Despite showing a fairly solid movement from the party's 1992 position, it nonetheless reflects similarities with its scores from the early 1970s and 1980s. At the same time, the Conservative Party was still to the left of the British score of 25.75 (Bara and Budge 2001). The Liberal Democrats present a pattern that seems to mirror Conservative movement. At times when the Conservative Party shifted towards the centre of the political spectrum, the Liberal Democrats did likewise, although when the Conservatives moved to the right the Liberal Democrats generally swung to the left of the political spectrum, a pattern repeated in 2010. The Liberal Democrats maintain the emerging pattern for Scottish politics during the period in question. A direct comparison between their British and Scottish scores in 1997 demonstrates a similar picture to that of the other two parties. In 1997 the Scottish Liberal Democrats' left–right score was –9.72, while their British score was –5.86 (Bara and Budge 2001). In 2010, when Scottish MP Charles Kennedy, the former leader of the Liberal Democrats, was the only member of the parliamentary party not to vote in favour of the Westminster coalition with the Conservatives, he may have been more in tune with his Scottish party than with the federal one.

For most of the last forty years the Scottish manifesto left–right scores were different from their British counterparts. There were only five occasions during this period when the British scores were to the left of their Scottish counterparts. On three occasions, 1979, 1983 and 1992, British Labour returned a score to the left of Scottish Labour, although all were within three percentage points. In 1979 the British Liberal manifesto was significantly to the left of the Scottish version. Likewise, in 1970, the British Conservative manifesto was to the left of its Scottish counterpart. Apart from these exceptions the Scottish manifestos have consistently placed Scottish parties to the left of their British equivalents.

Another emerging aspect of the pattern is the convergence occurring in the 2005 elections. At no other point during the last forty years have the parties all been moving towards a median point at the centre of the political spectrum. While the SNP and Labour tend to have similar patterns of shift, other parties have been moving in opposite directions at the same time. The 2005 election presents a very different picture for Scottish politics, with the difference between the most distant parties (the SNP and the Scottish

Conservatives) dropping to fewer than fifteen points on the left–right scale. The overall difference between the SNP and the Liberal Democrats was only 4.25, with the Labour Party between them on the scale. Scottish politics saw three of the four major parties all grouped around a similar point on the political spectrum, a situation never before witnessed. This may indicate that Scottish politics was following a trend identified by Downs (1957), although the 2010 results indicate the limitations of that conver- gence. From a point where three of the major parties had come together, a clear divergence has emerged, with the SNP heading into territory it has not occupied since the 1970s, and Labour in Scotland maintaining a left-of- centre position, a pattern repeated by the Liberal Democrats. However, the Conservatives, the fourth party of Scottish politics with only one MP, are once again in government at Westminster (albeit in coalition with the Liberal Democrats) despite their renewed emphasis on right-wing policies and being the outrider of mainstream Scottish politics.

Unionism versus Nationalism Policy Emphasis

We have ascertained that the parties in Scotland can be differentiated on a left–right scale in terms of both the inter-party and the intra-party (at the British level) position, and differing policy foci also indicate diverse attitudes and policy direction among the parties. This is even more obvious in an analysis of how the parties highlight and frame their policies on such issues as devolution and the Union, and how they emphasis and employ national identity.

Table 3.1 provides information that relates to two specific points in Scotland's recent political history. In both the 1979 and the 1997 devolution referenda, differences did exist with regard to the relationship between the manifestos and the referenda. The 1979 General Election was held after the 1979 referendum on devolution and thus the manifestos were produced after the result of that referendum. The events surrounding the referendum together with the actions of members of the Labour Party and of the SNP, certainly assisted in bringing about the 1979 election.

On the other hand, Labour announced its intentions to hold a refer- endum on devolution well before the 1997 elections were called (Gay 2004). The party had been involved in the Scottish Constitutional Convention and was formally committed to the establishment of a Scottish parliament. This position was later tempered with the qualification of an advisory referendum. Nevertheless, in both cases timing did impact on the content of the manifestos and on the nature of that content. The parties would obviously still reference policies on devolution and their attitude to the

Union between Scotland and England. An analysis of these policies, and expressions that refer to Scottishness and Britishness, allows us to define the overall stance of each party with regard to national identity and nationalism.

Table 3.1 Nationalist–unionist policies 1979 and 1997

Year	Party	Union +	Union –	Devo +	Devo –
1979	Con	1.80	0	0.40	0
1979	Lab	0.66	0	1.66	0
1979	L/Dem	0	0	4.17	0
1979	SNP	0	11.00	0	0
1997	Con	3.71	0	0	6.96
1997	Lab	0.56	0.11	2.62	0.11
1997	L/Dem	0	0	3.22	0
1997	SNP	0	6.55	0	0.53

Note: Because the 1979 data for the SNP is unavailable (no complete copies of the 1979 SNP manifesto have been located), the 1983 scores have been substituted instead.

The most obvious result on the issue of Union is the minimal attention to the subject provided by the majority of parties in their manifestos. Discussion within the documents is lacking, indicating limited commentary within the national political debate, or very one-sided comments at best, as, unsurprisingly, the SNP records the highest reported value at any one time. In fact, at most elections the SNP maintains negative commentary regarding the Union, although it became noticeably less negative in focus over time. When the other parties do discuss the Union their statements are negligible. The Liberal Democrats provide no stance at all, giving neither positive nor negative support, although in 1979 there was a strong positive focus on devolution. Their policy statements on that issue far outweighed the emphasis given by any other party at that time.

The Conservatives and Labour have consistently supported the Union but that support has also been very limited in their manifestos, as has been any support for devolution. No party has consistently and directly attacked devolution, although the Conservatives did give a focused emphasis on the negative aspects of devolution in 1997, but this remained an isolated event. Even the SNP, so strongly opposed to the Union, did not overtly challenge devolution, noting only the limitations of such a move versus independence. Such a stance is indicative in light of the outcome of the 1979 referendum vote. Despite failing to meet the requirements for passage, the vote indicated a level of support for devolution among Scottish voters, and there was little political capital in openly challenging the policy. Thus, other than from the Liberal Democrats, support for devolution was minimally present in 1979.

In 1997 the Conservatives continued to lead and increase their support for the Union, while at the same time increasing their opposition to devolution, although this did little to aid them at the ballot box. The Liberal Democrats again offer the most balanced policy on the Union simply by not having one: in 1997 they had no expressed policy statements for or against. They have traditionally been supporters of a federally structured UK, and their policy focus has been the need for devolution as opposed to dissolution. Such a stance was reflected in the level of policy statements given over to devolution, which continued to make them the leading party in this area; their 3.22 per cent score indicates that it remained a core policy and put them ahead of any other party, even Labour, who would deliver the policy while in government.

The SNP continued to present considerable levels of policy statements against the Union in 1997. Although, as noted above, a reduction in negativity is evident, the overall policy stance had in fact changed. A lower emphasis on the negative aspects of the Union indicated a rhetorical mitigation on the issue, which reflected the party's somewhat ambivalent political position of the time as regards constitutional change. While the SNP had withdrawn from the Scottish Constitutional Convention and did not formally support a Scottish parliament prior to the 1997 election, it openly encouraged support for the subsequent devolution referendum and a YES/YES vote. The 1997 manifesto content reflects this restrained attitude. The 6.55 per cent of the manifesto that openly challenged and attacked the Union was almost half the level recorded in 1979, and the very minimal 0.53 per cent of the manifesto that assailed devolution represents only token statements. Such limited negative statements reveal the ambivalence of the SNP at this time. While devolution is a half measure in the eyes of some of their supporters, and especially the more fundamental among the membership, the gradualists within the SNP saw it as 'a step in the right direction' and they have been in the ascendency (McGarvey and Cairney 2008).

The Labour Party presents the most widespread of policy statements in these areas. While Labour continued to emphasise limited support for the Union, its 1997 manifesto also included one negative statement towards it, a backhanded comment on the need for devolution. This is a similar picture to its policy on devolution. Labour had publicly committed itself to a referendum, and party policy was in favour of devolution. There were several positive policy statements within their manifesto, but it also contained one negative statement with regard to devolution. The support was therefore not total, and nor was Labour alone. Unlike in the 1970s, when no parties had negative policy statements with regard to devolution, in 1997 three parties indicated negativity, albeit for different reasons and objectives. Devolution was seen to have limitations from both the unionist and the Nationalist perspective. Even while supporting the policy of devolution, Labour expressed the primacy of the Union, the Conservatives attacked it as the first step on the road to independence and the SNP came from the opposite tack, seeing it as a sop against independence. Only the Liberal Democrats were fully in favour.

A NATIONALISM INDEX

The use of specific categories to analyse manifestos in a sub-state, national arena allows for the creation of a nationalism index that temporally measures the stance of the parties in relation to nationalism as a political goal. As with the left–right spectrum, coding categories emphasising support for greater autonomy, devolution or independence are added together, as are policy statements supporting the Union, or challenging devolution or independence. The latter are then subtracted from the former, with a negative score representing a unionist position and a positive one representing a nationalist stance. Although, theoretically, a party could score 100 per cent in either direction (if it produced a totally Nationalist or totally Unionist manifesto), what we are able to ascertain is a range of scores that indicate a general pattern across time and between parties. Therefore, while support for devolution registers as a positive on the scale, it does not reflect a separatist position. Rather, the score indicates a position between the two extreme and theoretically pure constitutional preferences and allows party preferences to include those ranging from the pre-devolution status quo (extreme Unionist), to some form of sub-state autonomy (devolution), to a most extreme sub-state autonomy (devo-max as it is sometimes known), through to dissolution of the Union (Separatist). Of course, this does not preclude a party supporting devolution because it considers it the best way to preserve the Union (for example, the Labour Party). Equally, the Conservative Party can argue that the best national Scottish interest lies in the situation as it exists now, without any further devolution of powers, thus gaining a minimal nationalist score due to expressed support for devolution. However, we would expect this to be offset by strongly expressed support for the Union, which is often the case. As a result, during the last forty years, parties in Scotland have adopted differing stances on such issues as the creation of a Scottish parliament, although to a degree each individual party has maintained a standardised position within the Scottish political system on the nationalism index.

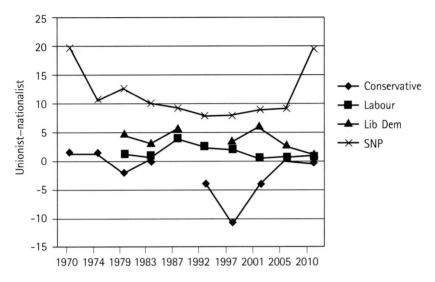

Figure 3.2 Nationalism index

The lack of 'leapfrogging' or notable alteration between parties indicates the stable nature of Scottish politics in this respect. The results demonstrate that the SNP has always been the most forceful on the nationalist–unionist spectrum and has continually been the outlier when compared to the other parties with regard to a pro-nationalist position. Equally, the Conservative Party has always maintained the least nationalist position, having spent the majority of the period with a firmly unionist score. The most stable of the major parties has been the Labour Party, whose score has remained in single digits during the period, and in this it was joined by the Liberal Democrats; both have had a low-level nationalist stance, although the Liberal Democrats have always scored a slightly more nationalist score than Labour. Despite this standard positioning there have been significant intra-party changes.

The SNP presented an initially extreme position in 1970, achieving an overall nationalism score of 19.59, which means that almost one-fifth of its manifesto provided policy statements dedicated to achieving political independence for Scotland, although the party tempered its position very significantly during the 1970s. At the October 1974 General Election, in which the party gained its highest-ever share of the vote, the nationalist score had almost halved to 10.47. Although this score rose again slightly in the early 1980s, the downward trend would continue after that point. By 1987 the party stood just slightly above a score of 10, and it maintained a position within two points of that score until 2010. The election at which the SNP produced its minimum nationalist index score was 1997, when all parties were aware that a devolution referendum was coming, having been promised this by the Labour Party in the event of it forming the government after the election. The SNP probably saw little need to further emphasise a nationalist stance to any potential supporters. The establishment of a Scottish parliament would provide a political arena in which it could reasonably hope to form the main opposition and seek to springboard to the next level – independence.

This moderation of the SNP on the index, which may have represented a softening of the Nationalist party's stance on independence, underwent a reversal at the 2010 election. During the previous five elections, the SNP had dedicated less than 10 per cent of each manifesto towards the core policy of independence, but in 2010, the party more than doubled that, with 19.64 per cent. Since the 1970s the SNP has continued to dedicate a good percentage of its manifesto towards nationalist policies; however, for the past three decades, it has significantly lessened this emphasis. Although the party remained focused on independence, tempering the position on the index was the policy support expressed for devolution in more recent SNP manifestos. By 2010, however, that tempering had dissipated and the SNP proudly proclaimed that independence 'runs like a golden thread throughout' the manifesto; a statement that made the party position emphatic. Once again, it seems that the SNP's historic 2007 Scottish Parliament electoral victory provided it with a firm foundation on which it would build, restate and re-emphasise its objective of independence for Scotland. The SNP, in government in Scotland, has consistently discussed independence as a policy objective. It produced a Scottish Government Green Paper, held a 'National Conversation' with the Scottish populace and chose to put that policy at the very heart of the most recent manifesto, reversing an evident historical trend. Within the context of the most recent British General Election, the SNP has chosen a most forceful, more fundamental position on independence.

At the other end of the scale, as the most unionist of parties, the Conservative Party also presents a mixed picture over time. From a mildly nationalist position in the early 1970s, with a score of 1.19 in 1970 and 1.28 in 1974, the Conservatives dropped into unionist territory later in the decade, recording –2.2 in 1979. This represents the change from supporting devolution and some form of Scottish 'assembly' in the 1970s to a more intransigent and anti-devolution position. As Margaret Thatcher became leader and the party headed into the 1979 election, this support was removed, and the limited unionist position re-emerged. Despite a short step back into the nationalist sphere in 1983, the Conservatives began to trend significantly into unionist territory. This continued trend was to result in the party recording a level of –11.14 in 1997, reflecting its outright opposition to any alteration to the existing UK constitutional structure. The party was firmly opposed to devolution and strongly supported the Union. These factors and specific policy statements combined to produce the most negative nationalist score reported by any party, a position that rapidly reversed after devolution became a political fact.

After the 1997 referendum the Conservatives openly acknowledged the widespread public support for devolution within Scotland; they recognised that opposition to devolution was not going to aid them in regaining electoral support within Scotland, and a less unionist stance emerged. In 2001, the Conservative score was –3.92, indicating that the party had not wholeheartedly embraced more nationalist policies within the manifestos, and negative statements attacking devolution and independence outweighed limited statements of support for the Scottish Parliament. Nevertheless the Conservatives achieved very limited nationalist scores in 2005, at 0.29 per cent, and although in 2010 they had moved to the other side of the spectrum again, it was only to record a unionist score of –0.43, a shift of less than 1 per cent. While Conservative support for devolution was never overwhelming, the party has begun to provide more statements specifically embracing a sense of Scottishness; rather than showing support for specific policies, however, it reflects a change in tone and rhetoric.

The Labour Party has maintained the most stable and minimal score on the nationalism index. From 1979 through to 2010 the score for the party that would deliver devolution has remained within a very narrow band. It has ranged from 1.16 per cent in 1979 to 3.81 per cent in 1987, the party's highest-ever recorded score on the index, and has been on a steady decline ever since. After devolution the Labour manifestos' emphasis on both the Union and devolution has remained relatively balanced and extremely minimal. During the last decade, Labour has remained in nationalist territory on the index, but has had scores ranging from 0.52 per cent in 2001 to 0.9 per cent in 2010. Open statements in favour of unionist or nationalist positions are extremely rare within the manifestos. Considering that it was Labour that 'delivered' devolution as a policy while in government, this position may surprise, but Labour's hegemonic position in

Scotland provides an explanation for such emphasis. Furthermore, recent evidence suggests that the Scottish electorate behaves differently at Westminster and Holyrood elections, favouring Labour at the former. As 'Scotland's establishment party' (Irvine 2004) Labour has long maintained its dominant position in General Elections in Scotland, and outside of specific times of challenge by the SNP (such as the early 1970s, which prodded Labour back into producing consistently Scottish manifestos) it has never felt the need to play the 'nationalist' card at British election time.

The Liberal Democrats have consistently maintained a higher level on the index than Labour while also, apart from in 2001, following a roughly analogous pattern. In 1979, the Liberal Democrat score of 4.37 per cent placed the party between Labour and the SNP, a position it has maintained since. The persistently more nationalist score on the index for the Liberal Democrats compared to Labour stems mainly from their continued and steadfast support for the policy of devolution. This has been a feature of Liberal Democrat manifestos for much of the period. The major difference with Labour in 2001, when the Liberal Democrat score was 5.93 per cent (ten times that of Labour), was a direct result of the proportion of the Liberal Democrats' manifesto given over to this policy. With regard to other aspects of the debate, they provide almost negligible policy statements, and since devolution has been delivered, the party remains focused on other policy areas. Indeed, it has remained very 'quiet' on certain issues that the other parties engage with on a regular basis.

An apparent emerging trend in the nationalism index is a convergence between the major parties, with the exception of the Nationalist SNP. The three major parties of both Scottish and British politics have, during the last ten years, consistently recorded minimal scores, closely grouped around the zero of the index. In 2010, the range has been only 1.53 per cent, and while Labour has maintained this neutral position, the Conservatives and the Liberal Democrats have softened their already minimal stances of the late 1990s. The SNP actually increased its nationalist stance while other parties converged on the centre. Nor has such a trend been a recent, post-devolution development. During the late 1980s and early 1990s, the parties all began to trend closer together, although the 1997 election reversed this to some extent. Including the period after 1997, the Conservative scoring on the nationalism index even at –11.44 per cent was much closer to that of the other parties. The gap that then existed between all the major political parties was less than 9 per cent, an historically narrow band over the last forty years of four-party politics but one that would continue to shrink.

The 2010 General Election saw any four-party convergence disappear. The SNP refocused on independence as a policy issue, which, when added to its continued support for enhanced devolution, took the party signifi-cantly away from the other three 'unionist' supporters. The three major Scottish/British parties all remain tightly grouped around the mid point of the scale and all provide support for both the Union and devolution at British election time, yet only very limited attention is given in their manifestos to either area. The Scottish political system, when operating within a British focus, seems to have returned to a pre-devolution position, with the Nationalists operating at a significant distance from the unionists, and the unionists emphasising a mildly 'nationalist-neutral' position.

Conclusions

The political landscape has changed significantly during the past forty years. The 1970 election took place with the SNP a minor party of Scottish politics, the Liberal Democrats a distant third and the two major parties of British politics, Labour and the Conservatives, taking the lion's share of votes and only 6.5 per cent apart in the polls. In 2010 the Westminster election resulted in Labour confirming its dominant position in Scotland, at the British level, with all other parties well behind in the polls. However, while the SNP was a distant second in vote share (but third in seats with only six MPs), it remained the party of Scottish government, having beaten Labour in the polls in 2007. Furthermore, the Liberal Democrats, with eleven MPs, maintained second place in seats, although the vote share dropped below that of the SNP, placing the party only 2 per cent ahead of the Conservatives, whose slightly similar vote share had gained a sole Scottish MP. It has been the Con-servatives who have suffered the most during the last four decades, and the party now stands as the fourth party of Scottish politics. Yet it is the Conservative Party in coalition with the Liberal Democrats that forms the government of the UK. Labour, although dominant in Scotland, finds itself outside of government in Scotland and in the UK.

In 2010 all parties sensed some possibility of victory to a greater or lesser extent, although the results only confirmed Labour's electoral dominance in Scotland. It is during these elections over the past forty years that parties have presented policies that directly impact on the nature of Scotland, its relationship with the rest of the UK, and thus the sense of national identity held by individuals within Scotland. Each party has sought to project not just an ideological or political identity for prospective supporters, but also a national identity alongside and intertwined with the political. National identity has been an integral part of the political system, a mainstay of all the major political party platforms, reflecting and interacting with their political and constitutional stance.

At the same time the parties have been quick to react to the results of elections. The fall in the number of Conservative MPs in Scotland to zero in 1997 saw a subsequent shift in position on the nationalism index. Likewise, a continued drop in Conservative support, to fourth place in the last three General Elections, had seen the party shift towards a more central point on the Scottish political spectrum until the last General Election. The recent patterns of left–right convergence indicated that all the parties were operating within a much more narrow range, although these trends have now reversed, with the SNP moving closer to the Conservative position and away from Labour and the Liberal Democrats. Not only was this narrowing an aspect of the left–right index, it was also apparent on the nationalism index. The location of the parties within the debate on national identity and nationalism, as shown in Figure 3.2, appeared less extreme in the last decade than was the case forty years ago, but has now reverted to a much earlier pattern. Today, we are in a changed political and constitutional structure but with a nationalism position that reflects the 1970s more than the 1990s or 1980s.

In purely political terms it has been argued that the Scottish electorate considers itself more working-class and left-wing than its English counterparts. Most of the political parties have presented policy platforms that are in agreement with this and, during the last four decades, the major parties have presented a more left-wing stance than was evident in the British manifestos. However, as the wider political spectrum of the UK has shifted towards the centre-right, the centre of Scottish politics has also shifted. Although the Scottish parties remain further to the left than their English counterparts, all have moved to the centre-right as well, including the SNP. Today the two political parties representing the outliers in the nationalist-unionist debate, the Conservatives and the SNP, can now be found on the same side of the left–right political spectrum, with the other two major parties closely grouped in the centre-left.

The parties have also presented a much closer relationship on national identity issues. In an age of devolution politics, all the major parties now engage positively with the policy of devolution. Differences still exist but the parties that support the Union remain close together, while the Nationalist SNP seems to be returning to a more fundamental stance. This has occurred at a time when the vote share between the parties has also become increasingly balanced, with Labour dominant and the others all within a small percentage distance of each other. Open expressions of Scottish national identity at British elections remain limited among unionists and Nationalists alike. There are few expressions or direct policy statements expressing a distinct sense of either Scottishness or Britishness. Uses of explicit identity-related statements, even among the most openly Nationalist and unionist of parties, are conspicuous by their absence, even while policies supporting independence or the continuation of the Union are evident.

While the CMP coding scheme provides a tool that produces a robust and valid series of measurements of manifestos, it does have limitations for our study. One of the major strengths of the coding scheme has allowed for a measurement of nationalism inherent in the manifestos and a consideration of inter- and intra-party movement. The approach provides an ability to consider policy changes within and between the major political parties. However, the rigid nature of the statistical analysis limits interpretation, which is why we have, in places, commented on the rhetoric and tone of specific language. Many of the comments within the manifestos, while focusing on a specific policy area, were constructed in a style or idiom that provided an extra dimension or nuance important to any consideration of nationalist language. Although the statement in question refers to a specific policy and is thus coded within that policy category, its rhetorical nature means that it could be informative to any consideration of national identity or nationalism and though this certainly does not negate the results presented here, it illustrates the need for greater rhetorical investigation. How the political parties utilise senses of Scottishness and Britishness within their campaign documents, portraying those identities to the Scottish electorate, requires further analysis. While the overall substance has been measured, a study of the nuances and discourse within manifestos may provide further insight into the nature of national identity, as envisaged and employed by the Scottish political parties. Furthermore, the rules of the political system, and the arena in which the game is played, have changed. As the events of 2010 have illustrated, Labour, the dominant party of elections from Scotland, is the only major party within Scotland that is not represented in government. The SNP forms the devolved government of Scotland, while the Liberal Democrats and the Conservatives form the coalition government of the UK. The last forty years of discussion have taken place from Scotland, but the last decade has seen a discussion that has taken place solely within Scotland. However, mapping explicit policy statements onto national identity is not the only way to explore the nationalist discourse of Scottish politicians, and so the next chapter will employ a supplementary discursive methodology.

4

Nationalism's Metaphor: the Discourse and Grammar of National Personification

INTRODUCTION

Social and political change over the last forty years has altered the role national identity plays in Scottish politics, particularly when Scottishness is measured against Britishness over the same period. This chapter continues to explore how language is used to represent Scotland within the electoral discourse contained in the manifestos of devolved Scottish politics. The previous chapter introduced for the first time a measurement for national identity similar to other policy preferences measurable on a left–right spectrum. With the increasing emphasis on Scottish national identity, it is legitimate to ask what these ideological interpretations of Scotland look like. How do the different parties construct Scotland in their discourse? For example, it has been asserted that Labour and the SNP have been successful, at least in recent times, in linking in the public mind centre-left social democratic values with Scottish national identity to the extent that right-wing Conservatism has often been associated with Englishness. As such, the Scottish Conservatives find themselves ideologically isolated in Scotland (McCrone 2001). Here we examine how the four major parties of Scotland draw on any civic and non-civic sources in their conceptions of the Scottish nation and Scottish national identity. The analysis will explore statements from the manifestos in more detail to investigate the character of these discursive constructions of Scotland and Scottish national identity. In particular, we will look at the linguistic phenomenon of the metaphorical personification of the nation and its banal discursive manifestations.

We begin with an extract from First Minister Alex Salmond's first speech outside Scotland, given to the Northern Ireland Assembly at Stormont on 18 June 2007.

Mr Speaker, the prevailing mood in my country is one of optimism and opportunity . . . Scotland is restless for change and keen to expand its influence and to reach out beyond our shores. That was the message we took to the Scottish people and that is the agenda we now lead . . . I don't stand before you as the First Minister of an independent Scotland – that must wait for another day perhaps.

But Mr Speaker, I do stand before this assembly as a Scottish First Minister determined to maximise every opportunity to promote the Scottish national interest.

Though the event of Scotland's first Nationalist First Minister speaking outside of and for Scotland for the first time might be novel enough, the language that Alex Salmond uses is not particularly novel or striking. That is not to say that the speech he gave was not well constructed and well delivered, but the language used is quite familiar to us, full of the tropes of high office, made in the formal style of parliamentary speeches, the honorific 'Mr Speaker' and 'First Minister', and impregnated with a leader's assumption to speak of and for their country. It is on this last point that we will focus: Salmond's speaking for and of his country and specifically how he did this.

If we take the short extract above and look at the references to Scotland, we see there are straightforward references to 'Scotland' and 'the Scottish people', where the country and its people are explicitly named. There are labels attached to other entities, denoting them as Scottish, as in 'Scottish First Minister' and 'Scottish national interest'; and there are small deictic references, such as pronouns, where 'my country' and 'its' elliptically mark Scotland in the speech. All these features of political speaking are very familiar to us, so much so that they are hardly noticed and nor do they seem important. Similarly, when Salmond says 'Scotland is restless for change and keen to expand its influence and to reach out', or speaks of 'an independent Scotland' or 'the Scottish national interest' nothing strikes us as particularly unusual. But if we look more closely and ask ourselves how Scotland is being referred to in these examples, we see a figure emerge: the nation in human form ascribed the sentient states of 'restlessness' and 'independence', having mental 'interests' and performing actions in 'reaching out'. There is a naturalness in speaking about a nation in this way; we are used to hearing our nations referred to as people. This is referred to by linguists as metaphorical personification (or simply personification) and is a linguistic process whereby some inanimate thing, or phenomenon, is anthropomorphised through the use of metaphor and given human qualities (Shelestiuk 2006). For example, in the following extracts from the same speech the elements constructing metaphorical personification are italicised:

We identified then that the time is ripe for Scotland and Northern Ireland *to renew our engagement* . . .

This is the best mechanism we currently have for Scotland and Northern Ireland *to work together* within the devolved structure.

And *together*, our nations *have borne the forces* of history.

Salmond reiterates to the debating chamber Scotland and Northern Ireland's historical connection and potential for future collaboration, and in doing so the two nations are cast as people renewing an 'engagement' and who can 'work together'. People can work together, but inanimate objects and abstract political bodies cannot, and so Scotland and Northern Ireland are imbued with the human ability to perform actions.

Metaphorical personification has a long provenance in political language and imagery: 'Victorian editions of the *London Gazette* symbolise the nations of Europe either by caricatures of actual leaders (e.g. Napoleon) or mythical ones (e.g. John Bull)' (Charteris-Black 2005: 204). Nations are commonly thought of as a metaphorical family, which is why different nations think of their country as the 'motherland' or 'fatherland', and we speak of sending our 'sons' and 'daughters' off to war. Other personifications include the figure of Britannia with shield and trident in hand, and the encompassing figure of the King on the frontispiece of Hobbes' *Leviathan* as the embodiment of the body-politic arising unified to bring order out of the state of nature. While the images and tropes of anthropomorphised nations are familiar, personification has received little attention in studies of political discourse and nationalism.[1] Charteris-Black (2004; 2005) has given personification detailed attention in his analysis of metaphor in political speechmaking. He comments that personification in political discourse 'evokes our attitudes, feelings and beliefs about people and applies them to our attitudes, feelings and beliefs about political entities' (Charteris-Black 2005: 41). In an analysis of Winston Churchill's oratory Charteris-Black demonstrates the prominence of personification in the Prime Minister's wartime rhetoric and its importance as an ideological tool. Elaborating on ideological uses he notes:

Typically, the ideological basis for using personification is either to arouse empathy for a social group, ideology or belief evaluated as heroic, or to

[1] The phenomenon has been discussed in general terms, in semantic theory (Taylor 1995) and most notably in the seminal works on metaphor theory by Lakoff (1987) and Lakoff and Johnson (1980). Lakoff's Moral Politics (2002) demonstrates how conceptual metaphors underpin moral reasoning in American politics.

arouse opposition towards a social group, ideology or belief that is evaluated as villainous. This is done by associating social groups, ideologies and beliefs that are positively evaluated with heroic human attributes – such as courage and determination – and by associating negatively evaluated social groups, ideas etc. with villainous attributes – such as cowardice and treachery. (2005: 41)

This analysis is, however, of a strong wartime leader prosaically rallying the nation in times of international peril. We would like to draw attention to the less noticeable, more banal occurrences of personification in political discourse and, more particularly, how metaphorical personification and the connected phenomenon of metonymy contribute to the discourse of nationalism. An accessible outline of metaphor and metonymy and how they relate to a study of nationalist discourse will be given below before we move on to a Scottish specific analysis.

Metaphor and Language

The traditional view of metaphor is that it is something out of the ordinary in the normal ebb and flow of language, and that it is the dramatic tool of poets and master orators, in which one thing is characterised as another thing, as in *life is a journey* or *Juliet is the sun*. Kövecses notes of this view of metaphor:

> We would probably also say that the word is used metaphorically in order to achieve some artistic and rhetorical effect, since we speak and write metaphorically to communicate eloquently, to impress others with 'beautiful,' aesthetically pleasing words, or to express some deep emotion. (2002: vii)

However, as we have already noted, metaphors of the type 'the nation is a person' are very familiar to us, so much so that they typically do not strike us as particularly 'eloquent', 'beautiful' or 'aesthetically pleasing'. In fact, the current dominant theory of metaphor, conceptual metaphor theory (CMT), views metaphor in quite different terms. First developed by Lakoff and Johnson (1980), the theory suggests that metaphors are an essential part of creating meaning in language, play an important role in our conceptualisation and reasoning processes, and, far from being the province only of exceptional poets and politicians, are used by everyone every day. In this theory the conceptual aspect of metaphor is distinct from the occurrence of a metaphor in actual language. As such, the convention exists in CMT to indicate the conceptual level of the metaphor in block capitals and the textual example italicised in lower case, which is the convention followed from now on.

Metaphor is particularly useful to speakers of a language when needing to speak about abstract concepts or things. For example, speakers of English use a set of highly conventionalised metaphors for speaking about time. Time is understood in terms of physical space, the future being in front of us (e.g. *looking ahead to the future*), the past far away (e.g. *the distant past*) and the present near. Time is also understood as movement through space (e.g. *time flies on*) and as a journey (e.g. *time's passage*). There are many other important abstract concepts reliant on metaphor, including: LOVE IS A JOURNEY (e.g. *our marriage is at a crossroads*), THE MIND IS A MACHINE (e.g. *the workings of her mind*), RELATIONSHIPS ARE BUILDINGS (e.g. *a relationship with strong foundations*), MORE IS UP (e.g. *I got a pay rise*). In a similar vein, nations are conventionally conceptualised as people in the metaphor THE NATION IS A PERSON, and because this meaning is so conventionalised in a world of nations we rarely notice it, let alone think it significant.

In congruence with the SCOTLAND IS A PERSON metaphor are cases of metonymy. This is a process of transferred reference whereby one thing which is considered as being from the same semantic field of reference can stand for something else in the field (Taylor 1995: 122). For example 'the White House today delivered a response to recent criticisms' is an example of metonymy in which 'the White House' is able to stand for a range of possible agents, such as the press office of the Presidency or the entire executive branch of the USA. In our examples Scotland sometimes stands for Scotland the person as well as for the Scottish people. Or, taking an example from Alex Salmond's speech above, 'Scotland is restless for change and keen to expand its influence and to reach out beyond our shores'. Initially, Scotland appears as a person 'restless for change' but then the metaphor of the person changes to a metonymy of 'our' national shores'. This example highlights the issue of reference: what is it that Scotland, whether metaphor or metonymy, is referring to? What does the 'Scotland' signify? The answer is so commonsensical that it need not be made explicit – it is Scotland the place and its people, for there cannot be one without other; there are no nations without people. Therefore, even if the metaphorical personification or metonymy that signifies 'Scotland' is the same, the method of signification is different. The proximity of the two different methods of reference illustrates how personification is a conventionalised trope of nationalist discourse which refers to the same thing: Scotland the place, which is coterminous with Scotland the people. The combination of these two linguistic forms of reference, metaphor and metonymy, support each other (Culler 1981: 206). The very basis of the sense of the SCOT-LAND IS A PERSON metaphor is premised on the existing cultural knowledge that such a national body exists and that 'we' the Scottish people have ways of denoting 'our' existence discursively, be that deictically (that is grammatically) referring to 'us', 'ours' and 'here', metonymically as 'Scotland' standing for 'the people of Scotland', 'the Scottish Government' or 'Scotland the place', or metaphorically as Scotland the personified embodied nation.

As mentioned in Chapter 1, Anderson (2006) and Billig (1995) have explored the 'imagined' nature of modern nations and the significance of discursive acts in creating and maintaining nations and nationalisms. In Billig's (1995) thesis of 'banal nationalism' (1995) the idea and reality of a nation is maintained day to day by small habitual discursive acts routinely flagging the nation in, for example, political and media discourse through the use of words such as 'our', 'us' or 'here' deictically pointing to 'our' nation. Rather than focusing on grammatical deixis, we will demonstrate how the nation is personified and how nationalist discourse moves with ease between the metaphor THE NATION IS A PERSON and the metonymy of 'our' Scotland. In turn, we will use this analysis to illustrate what type of nation Scotland is discursively and routinely constructed to be in devolved Scottish politics.

Much of the work done in this discursive tradition so far has focused on the national press, including Scottish-specific work (Higgins 2004a, 2004b; Law 2001; Petersoo 2007; Rosie et al. 2004). However, our analysis takes on the role of political parties in the discursive processes of constructing the nation, with particular emphasis on manifesto statements of the four main parties of Scotland during all three devolved elections since 1999. This chapter will first expand on the grammatical analysis of metaphor, illus-trating the ways in which Scotland is constructed as a person, laying the foundations for a discursive analysis engaging with our wider thesis on the civic–non-civic aspects of Scottish nationalism.

THE NATION AS METAPHOR

We identified the metaphor of THE NATION IS A PERSON through an analysis of grammar by looking at how Scotland is said to act as a person. Therefore, a grammar of personification would look at how, principally, verbs and adverbs in English encode the nation's different actions and states of being. The nation, when conceived as an entity, can be con-structed with types of verbs usually associated with human process types, specifically as in 'being' in a particular state, doing actions, thinking or speaking, and possessing an attribute or other thing. We will take each of these in turn.

Processes of 'Being'

These are indicated by the verb 'to be', which is usually of two types in English: attributive ('Scotland is small') and identifying ('Scotland is a world leader') (for further details on the grammatical analysis used here see Halliday and Matthiessen 2004). In the first example, smallness is an attributive characteristic of Scotland, whereas in the second example Scotland is identified as being a thing, in this instance 'a world leader'. Of course, in the first example Scotland being 'small' does not necessarily mean it is being characterised in human terms, whereas in the second example it is clearly being characterised in human terms. Any object can be small or large but not every object can be a leader because that is a human faculty; rocks do not lead. It is not always clear from short extracts whether personification is being employed, so sometimes the wider context must be taken into account. For example, 'Scotland is small in a world of burly multinational companies' is more clearly an instance of Scotland personified because of the sense given to multinational companies by the adjective 'burly'. Two instances of processes of 'being' are: 'a Scotland which *is proud* of its beautiful surroundings and rich history' (Labour 2007: 91) and 'Scotland *is restless* for change'.

The first example, from Labour's 2007 manifesto, shows Scotland with the human emotional state of pride; while in the second, an extract from Alex Salmond's Stormont speech, the nation is imbued with the agitated and impatient demeanour of a sentient being.

Processes of 'Doing' and 'Thinking'

Rocks most certainly do not perform actions and are not usually known for their thinking abilities; these are very much the domain of human beings. Of course animals perform actions, and traditionally personification is extended to cover describing inanimate objects and abstract phenomena as animals too. That being said, we found no examples of Scotland being personified as an animal, though the French cock, the Russian bear and the American eagle are examples of nations which are. In the manifestos, we find Scotland performing many different types of action, for example: 'Our country *stands at a crossroads*' (Labour 2007: 3); 'It's time for Scotland *to blaze a trail*' (Conservative 2007: 18).

With these processes of 'doing' Scotland is made a dynamic actor, poised to make a decision on which way to go and ready to forge ahead. But in the THE NATION IS A PERSON metaphor, these actions might also be premeditated with that most human of characteristics, thought, as in: 'Scotland *expects* and deserves its Parliament to deliver' (Conservative 2007: 3); 'Scotland must *learn* from those nations that came at the top of the UNICEF index of child wellbeing' (Liberal Democrat 2007: 10); and 'If Scotland *chooses* the SNP, we will implement a three year programme' (SNP 1999: 2). In observing the sentient mind of the nation one can see Scotland performing mental processes, 'learning' from experiences, 'choosing' between alternatives and having 'expectations' of its political institutions.

POSSESSION

As with thinking and certain forms of being and doing, possession is another human phenomenon, especially when it is the possession of other objects of human-like characteristics; a rock may literally 'have' rough edges, but only metaphorically can we say 'the Eiffel Tower *takes an imposing stance*'. Possession is indicated in several ways. There are verbs of possession, for example, 'Scotland also *has* the opportunity to lead the world in Carbon Capture and Storage' (Conservative 2007: 9), where the abstract concept of an 'opportunity' is something only sentient beings 'have'. Possession is also indicated by pronouns, such as 'its' or 'his', as in 'Scotland is restless for change and keen to expand *its* influence'. Pronouns tend to stand in for nouns with agency; if used to elliptically represent a phenomenon or an inanimate object they may therefore entail a metaphorical personification. And finally, there is the genitive inflection, or 'apostrophe s', for example, 'Scotland's diversity is a strength' (Labour 2003: 39) and 'Scotland's Party asks for Scotland's support to make Scotland's Parliament work' (SNP 1999: 1). In the first example of the genitive inflection, Scotland is described as being in possession of an animate attribute, 'strength', whereas in the second example Scotland is in possession of two 'things', a 'Party' and a 'Parliament'.

Such grammatical observations may seem quite inconsequential until it is considered that the nation and its people can therefore be constructed discursively as being, having, doing and thinking within the usual human moral and social categories. As Charteris-Black puts it:

Personifications provide a concrete and accessible framework for the evaluation of abstract political ideologies. They activate emotions originating in pre-existent myths about classes, nations and other social and ethnic groupings etc . . . In this respect personifications provide arche-typal political myths because they rely on pre-existent culturally rooted stereotypes to communicate emotionally potent and unambiguous eva-luations on an ethical scale of right and wrong. (2005: 204)

In the discourse of nationalism the ubiquity of the THE NATION IS A PERSON metaphor means that the nation is grounded in the same moral and political milieu as individual citizens. The nation, therefore, can be constructed in varying realisations of the human condition and in these differing forms one can see many diverse aspects of the nation. There are the inclusive civic conceptions, so often foregrounded by political parties and academics alike, such as education, the law, demographic diversity, and religious and social tolerance. In democracies, civic values tend to be inclusive because of the pluralistic and accountable nature of government and public culture. However, there can be exclusive civic forms as well, as societies are inherently bounded, making distinctions between themselves and others and assigning rights and responsibilities on that basis. Inclusive civic values would be religious tolerance or the universal right to education, whereas exclusive values would be prohibiting English residents from voting in devolved Scottish elections. There are also exclusive non-civic concep-tions; these include representations of the nation in terms of language, religion, landscape, history, place and tribe, some illustrations of which are also evident in Chapter 6. Exclusive, non-civic conceptions are ways of distinguishing one's nation from others on non-constitutional or legal grounds. In making distinctions, boundaries are created that indicate difference, boundaries which are, at some level of realisation, exclusive. In contrast are the former civic conceptions encoding meanings associated with democratic and civic values, like social diversity, inclusiveness and public institutions and practices. Therefore, excluding English residents from voting in Scotland is a civic value; excluding the English on the basis of their ethnic origin would be a non-civic value. However, non-civic values can also be inclusive, as in support of so called 'community languages'.

Constructing Scotland in Devolved Election Manifestos

As noted before, Scottish modernists tend to emphasise civic aspects of nationalism as prime in the politics of Scottish identity. Their argument has largely been premised by a heavy emphasis on civic society; in the absence of sovereign state apparatus, this distinctive Scottish civic society is claimed to have been kept alive through legal, educational and ecclesiastical institutions post-1707. Our analysis points to further evidence of the presence of non-civic aspects of national identity in the political discourse of Scottish politics. The previous consideration of the manifestos of the political parties gave us considerable insight into the political placement and social employment of a sense of national identity in Scottish politics. However, thus far we have not looked at manifestos as part of the wider socio-political discourse, which is part of the discursive *habitus* of constructing and referencing the nation. As such, the following qualitative discourse analysis takes a linguistically based grammatical approach to metaphor in order to better compare the detail and meanings of party political conceptions of Scotland and Scottish identity.

Billig (1995) and Shotter (1993) claim that nationalism is a tradition of argumentation concerning who the national 'we' is, and this argument is premised on certain elements that are taken for granted:

> Rival politicians and opposing factions present their different visions of the nation to their electorates. In order for the political argument to take place with the nation, there must be elements which are beyond argument. Different factions may argue about how 'we' should think of 'ourselves' and what is to be 'our' national destiny. In so doing they will take for granted the reality of 'us', the national place. (Billig 1995: 95–6)

These 'elements which are beyond argument' are evident in the construction of Scotland the place and Scotland the people, which political parties routinely use to address their audience. An important part of this process is the trope of personification.

The Discourse of Civic Nationalism

In this analysis of personification, we would expect to see that those things that make up the nation and make it distinctive – its institutions and its shared public ways of life – would be articulated as qualities of Scotland the person. This section will therefore demonstrate expressions of different realisations of nationalism, starting with civic nationalism in its inclusive and neutral forms that support the modernists' thesis. A modernist's Scotland would be a person of the type that embodies aspects of their civic nationalism, and this person would enter the political discourse of devolved manifestos repeatedly and in inclusive garb.

The following is undoubtedly civic: 'The first term of the Parliament has also given a *voice* to Scotland's civic society in a way missing during the Tory years' (Labour 2003: 40). Scotland possesses a 'civic society' which now has a 'voice' to speak in the world of politics. This is a society living the ideals of democracy: to have a place and the freedom to speak its mind. The denial of that right by the Conservatives during the 'Tory years' is given greater significance if it is the denial of an individual's voice; the importance of the individual's right to freedom and speech is metaphorically transferred to the target domain of Scottish civic society. Here, our collective Scottish voice moves with ease between metaphoric Scotland the person and the metonymic Scotland of 'us'.

In similar possessive tones, education is a defining characteristic of Scotland personified; compare the following:

Scotland*'s great achievements* have been built on the foundations of great education. It is still the case that a good education unlocks potential, expands horizons and leads to a positive contribution to a creative society. (SNP 1999: 6)

Scotland *has* a celebrated record of educating *its* citizens to a high standard. (Conservative 2007: 25)

Liberal Democrats want Scotland*'s* education system to be among the best in the world. (Liberal Democrats 1999: 5)

Education is framed by the personification metaphor in several ways. In the first example, Scotland's personal 'achievements' have been made possible by the metaphorical 'foundations' of its education system. In the second example Scotland possesses a celebrated record for personally educating, that is, metaphorically acting to educate its citizens. Most straightforwardly, as in the third example, the education system is a possession of Scotland. The education system is civically and inclusively defined, educating the citizenry and in turn releasing potential, but more significantly it is positively valued with an emotive vigour. One would not expect a dispassionate Enlightenment rationalism to bullishly exult the education system to be 'among the best in the world' and to be 'celebrated'; not only that, but the nation's 'great achievements' are the result of this 'great education'. The banality of personification occludes the nationalist ideological turn of extolling the nation's rational civic virtues. Similarly, in 'We are fiercely proud of Scotland*'s* unique legal system' (2007: 12) the Conservatives use the genitive inflection to denote the legal system as belonging to the embodied Scotland. However, the civic institution is unique, with its specificity ascribed to the character of Scotland and as something the people are emotively 'fiercely proud of'.

The plural, democratic character of Scottish nationalism cannot be denied; the organs of the distinctive Scottish civic society are there, embedded in the DNA of nationalist rhetoric, embodied in the public culture and in the institutions of Parliament, law and education. Indeed, the plurality is further acknowledged in electoral discourse, 'Scotland's diversity is a strength' (Labour 2003: 39); it is a physical power of the national body and it is a disposition of the nation's character:

Scotland *has always been an outward looking* nation. (SNP 2003: 24)

The SNP welcomes the contribution of Scotland's ethnic minorities to our national life. Scotland *has* a long tradition of *welcoming* those who choose to live here. (SNP 2003: 27)

Scottish Conservatives understand that diversity is one of Scotland's *defining characteristics* as a country. (Conservative 1999: 25)

Unionist and Nationalist together eulogise the progressive and 'welcoming' nature of the nation; this is the dual voice of a modernist democratic nationalism expressing its distinctive, unique character, but the nature of that character is an open, civic and inclusive plurality. It is both common to all and yet idiosyncratic in realisation, the universal voice of the Enlightenment realised in the particularity of a specific national political entity.

THE DISCOURSE OF NON-CIVIC NATIONALISM

The analysis now transitions to non-civic articulations of nationalism in devolved manifestos, the type which Scottish modernists would claim are not an important feature of Scottish nationalist discourse, but which, as we illustrate, are easy enough to identify in party political communication. These forms of nationalism centre on expressions associated with landscape, history, heritage, culture and tradition, which are said to be peculiar to Scotland, marking it out as different from other nations.

In referring to the national landscape, parties are constructing conceptions of Scotland the place. This geographical definition is non-civic as it does not pertain to either the political or the civic institutional practices of the polity. Landscape is a particularly exclusive definition of the nation as well, indicating boundaries and geographical specificity. For example, the Liberal Democrats, in the following extract, identify landscape as a key Scottish feature:

Rural Scotland is the jewel in Scotland's crown, providing the high quality food, glorious landscape, leisure opportunities and celebrated heritage that is central to the way our country is perceived and marketed around the world . . . Scottish Liberal Democrats believe that preserving and enhancing Scotland's rural areas and natural heritage is vital to Scotland's economic and social *wellbeing*. (2007: 68)

In this metaphor the landscape is an important characteristic of Scotland the person. The landscape is valuable, beautiful and essential to the health and wealth of a living Scotland. The initial personification is quite clear. '*Rural Scotland is the jewel in Scotland*'s crown': Scotland is a monarch and its countryside is the glimmering focal point of its anointed majesty, its landscape is 'glorious' and its heritage is 'celebrated'. Landscape is a non-civic element and here it is essential and something so precious which needs 'preserving and enhancing' in order to ensure the continued 'wellbeing' of the nation. The values we associated with human beauty and wellbeing, through the SCOTLAND IS A PERSON metaphor, are transferred onto the target domain of Scotland and its countryside. This is the nationalist value of the sacred bounded place given human form, and in the discourse of nationalism the nation is imbued with the emotional content of human life, which must be protected to ensure its continuation.

Similar emotive epithets are used to flag the homeland in patriotic and dramatic terms. In the 2003 manifestos Scotland's geography is variously described as 'unique' (Liberal Democrats 2003: 16), a 'beautiful country' (SNP 2003: 14) and possessing the 'most scenic landscapes in Europe' (SNP 2003: 19). This is not Scotland the democratically open society; it is Scotland of the glen and highland mist, of lochs and heather; it is the nation as the place of emotional belonging and geographical uniqueness. Here, 'our' nation is more beautiful than others and the national 'we' is coterminous with the landscape it inhabits.

Scottish culture is also personified as a positive aspect of Scotland's character, as in the following two extracts:

For a small country Scotland *has an immense reputation* for its literature, its artists, its music and its sport. Scotland's unique place in literary history was acknowledged when Edinburgh was named UNESCO's first World City of Literature. From Burns to Rankin, from Rennie Mackintosh to Maxwell Davies Scotland *has always punched above it[s] cultural weight*. (Labour 2007: 91)

The SNP recognises the importance of our national orchestras, opera and ballet companies in enhancing Scotland's *cultural reputation* and providing employment and training for musicians and artists. (SNP 1999: 27)

Both the SNP and Labour speak of Scotland's *'reputation'* for its culture, a reputation that extends beyond Scotland to the rest of the world. The personification goes further in Labour's extract, where Scotland is a prize fighter that *'has always punched above it[s] cultural weight'*. Personification is a rhetorical tool that constructs culture, whether it is literature or ballet, as a prized and integral characteristic of Scotland the individual. Metonymically, however, this is our Scottish reputation, our 'unique place in literary history' and the importance of our cultural institutions which make us and our country distinctive.

Finally, on non-civic articulations of Scottish nationalism, the invocation of national tradition, heritage, and history and language in the discourse of Scottish nationalism is attended to. The Liberal Democrats mark tradition as a possession of the nation: 'Scotland *has* huge natural assets, not least our tradition of enterprise and innovation' (1999: 15). The metaphorical personification moves to Scotland as a metonymy of the national collective: 'our tradition of enterprise and innovation' is framed as 'huge natural assets' of Scotland, organically part of the living nation. One might note, however, that this is not an ethnically or tribally defined tradition, but one of creativity and entrepreneurialism. Likewise, in the same manifesto 'Scotland *has* a strong tradition of internationalism, and a *proud* history of diplomatic and trading links around the world' (Liberal Democrats 1999: 32). Scotland has the human qualities of pride in and possession of its tradition and history, but this is an outward-looking tradition embracing 'internationalism' and pursuing external 'trading links'. There are other, more inward-looking embodiments of non-civic culture: 'We will recognise the importance of Gaelic as a unique part of Scotland's *national living heritage*' (Labour 2003: 37). The possession of Scotland, Gaelic, is personified as living history linking the past and present culture.

In these examples culture, tradition and history are variously and widely defined, and while they are non-civic in their definitions, their realisations in party political discourse are not straightforwardly inward-looking. The characterisation of Scotland's features is not a simple case of being predominantly civic or non-civic; nor is it a case of civic articulations being purely inclusive and outward-looking while the non-civic are not merely parochial and atavistic.

A MULTIPLE PERSONALITY

This chapter has continued the distinction between civic and non-civic aspects of society. However, in contemporary democracies, a strict distinction is not possible, as many aspects of what would be considered non-civic life are often subsidised or otherwise supported and regulated by the state. Sport, film and theatre, art and language all receive some form of state sponsorship in Scotland and the UK, whether in the form of tax breaks, direct subsidies and grants or forms of centralised administration. Just as Anderson (2006) suggested that there probably has never been a tidy fit between nations and states, so it is safe to assert that the boundaries between civic and non-civic aspects of society are not so easily drawn. Therefore, it is unsurprising to find expressions of nationalism evident in all the parties' devolved manifestos which seem inclusive yet bounded, or exclusive but pluralistic. The SNP wants to administer 'Scotland's culture and languages' (2003: 18) from a new department and to share this 'vibrant heritage, culture and creativity' (2003: 14) by promoting 'Scotland's distinctive culture internationally' (2007: 56). Labour suggests sport is 'an integral part of Scottish life and culture' (2007: 91) and that 'Scotland's culture . . . makes Scotland unique' (2003: 36). These conceptions balance differing definitions of the nation; they are at once exclusive in defining 'our' national culture but also often inclusive, suggesting that culture is diverse. We therefore find both civic and non-civic conceptions of Scottish nationalism, but the civic need not be purely inclusive nor the non-civic entirely exclusive. For example, the following two extracts illustrate how the geographically bounded place of Scotland can be simultaneously a place of treasured emotional belonging, a product to be marketed to others and a location of both topographic and demographic diversity:

Scotland's landscape is celebrated around the world. It is cherished by people across Scotland and is a major part of the tourism experience for many visitors to Scotland. It is important that we protect this natural asset. (Liberal Democrat 2007: 40)

Geographically, Scotland *is* a diverse nation, with some of the least densely populated and most scenic landscapes in Europe. As a nation, our strength is in that diversity. (SNP 2003: 19)

First, Scotland possesses the attribute of its landscape, its 'natural asset', which is admired within and beyond its borders. In the second, Scotland's geographical diversity is a condition of its being in the relational verb 'to be'. These two conceptions may be non-civic, but both are framed in terms of an open nationalism. In particular, the second example provides an illustration of a rhetorical turn which initially defines Scotland's geographical condition as one of diversity, but begins to shift in the following sentence from topographic variety to demographic diversity, the latter defined metaphorically in pluralistic and inclusive tones as national 'strength'. 'Our' topographical diversity mirrors 'our' demographic diversity and both are an attribute of the Scottish self.

The transition from landscape to cultural diversity can be seen again in Labour's 2007 manifesto and personification is once more the discursive tool used:

> Our vision is of *a confident and vibrant Scotland – a Scotland which is proud of its beautiful surroundings and rich history, but which also embraces the opportunities presented by change.* Scottish Labour remains committed to an inclusive Scotland, where everyone – no matter their background – shares in *Scotland's rich cultural and sporting heritage.* (Labour 2007: 91)

Scotland is personified as possessing the mental dispositions of confidence and pride, and as being physically vibrant and embracing opportunities. However, this is a vision for Scotland to be 'confident and vibrant' and 'proud' of its landscape, rich history, and cultural and sporting heritage. The richness of these national attributes is presupposed in Labour's statement but the implication is that Scotland is not yet confident and not yet self-assured enough to 'embrace the opportunities presented by change'; under Labour's stewardship, however, presumably it will be. The manifesto then moves to a statement of support for an inclusive approach to culture, landscape and heritage, 'where everyone – no matter their background – shares' in that 'rich cultural and sporting heritage'. The non-civic attributes of the nation are therefore defined in inclusive terms.

Language policy in the devolved manifestos provides another illustration of the complexity of civic and non-civic articulations of Scottish nationalism. In an inversion of the previous example, the initial proclamations appear inclusive and embracing of diversity, yet in specification they delimit boundaries. We have already indicated the importance given to language in creating a sense of national identity, and this importance is echoed in Scotland's political realm, evident in the parties' statements about the nation's languages. Consider the following personifications, both non-civic yet inclusive:

> *Scotland's* culture, from the languages we speak to the arts we perform and applaud, the sports we play and the riches we find in our libraries and museums, makes Scotland unique. (Labour 2003: 36)

> Scotland *has* a distinctive and colourful language heritage. Today in Scotland there are speakers of English, Scots, Gaelic, many community languages such as Chinese Urdu and British Sign Language. Language

enriches our entire society and allows citizens to access public services and communicate with each other. (Liberal Democrat 2003: 36)

Metaphorical possession of a 'distinctive' culture, of which 'language' is a part, makes the nation 'unique'. The manifestation of Scotland in the initial example is metonymic too, as Scotland is also the referent for 'languages we speak' which 'enrich our society'. All three of the centre-left parties, Labour, the Liberal Democrats and the SNP, proclaim that they will give institutional support to languages. They make positive and inclusive claims about Scotland's languages; they variously refer to English, Scots and Gaelic as well as to 'community languages' such as Urdu, Punjabi and British Sign Language. As in the example above, these languages manifest as paratactic lists of items of equivalent value. Viewed in these terms, the parties' attitudes to languages would be culturally inclusive. However, for the three centre-left parties some languages are 'more equal than others', a position that is nationalist in the non-civic sense. Labour states that Gaelic is part of Scotland's 'national living heritage' (2003: 37), and all three parties commit themselves to supporting Gaelic, while the Liberal Democrats and the SNP include Scots as a language worthy of state protection. To this end, the Liberal Democrats state: 'We will: Recognise the importance to Scotland's history and culture of our heritage languages of Gaelic and Scots' (2003: 36–7) and latterly, 'We will create a sustainable future for Gaelic in Scotland through the full implementation of the recently launched National Plan for Gaelic' (2007: 86). In 2003 the SNP promised to 'secure status for the Gaelic and Scots languages' (2003: 18) while only 'encouraging community languages' (2003: 18). However, by 2007 the SNP denoted 'Scotland's languages' only to refer to Scots and Gaelic, with no mention of other 'community languages'. In political, that is to say nationalist terms, one must assume that Scots and Gaelic are of more value than 'community languages'. Perhaps, then, it is to be implied that Scots and Gaelic are somehow more Scottish than other languages, as 'living heritage' would suggest, evoking a form of perceived temporal continuity and shared linguistic practice between countrymen. Although the manifestos across the political spectrum inclusively proclaim Scotland to have a diversity of languages and cultures, they also exclusively privilege two of those languages. Therefore, Scots and Gaelic are not so much languages found in Scotland as *the* Scottish languages.

CHARACTERISING SCOTLAND'S PERSONALITY

We have here taken an explicitly non-quantitative look at the politics of nationalism in order to get a sense of what the political parties of Scotland construct Scotland to be during Scottish elections. We have identified the conventionalised metaphor of THE NATION IS A PERSON in the political discourse, via an analysis of devolved manifestos, focusing on nationalist metaphors of the nation. Using a grammatical approach, we have seen that Scotland is frequently characterised as a person bearing different characteristics. What can the personality of Scotland the person said to be like, then? What defines the national character (at least, in political manifestos)? We have seen a nation personified, that is, a nation being and acting in different ways, and thinking and even saying different things, and this has told of the multifaceted character of Scotland. In the Bakhtinian (1981) sense, this is a discourse in which Scotland spoke with different conflicting voices, constructing itself as both pluralistic and democratic polity, and yet bounded, particular and atavistic. But where does this leave the wider discussion of studies into Scottish nationalism and national identity?

The non-civic conceptions of the nation and nationalism by Scotland's politicians sit at odds with modernists' arguments. McCrone suggests that 'The key to understanding Scotland lies in recognising that nationalism derives from . . . institutional autonomy, and is not some vague set of historic emotions which politicians can manipulate' (2001: 195). However, as McCrone's (2001) own study indicates, birth, ancestry and residence are considered the main markers of Scottishness by a majority of Scots. Scots are said to pragmatically choose civic democratic solutions for Scotland at elections (or referenda), and these pragmatic decisions override any non-civic, more emotive conceptions of nationalism. Therefore, civic nationalism must be the dominant conception of Scottish nationalism. However, at elections or referenda voters are asked to make a decision within the context of formal state institutions. Therefore, it is hardly unexpected that, given the civic context, voters make decisions which largely fulfil civic conceptions of national identity. These civic decisions are those that best fit the *habitus* of the democratic culture of which voters are a part. Given a cultural context, such as an international football match, the non-civic, exclusive conceptions of the nation and nationalism are paramount; here heritage, parentage, commonality of place of birth and language are much more important.

Though modernists emphasise that in Scotland nationalism is not something that politicians can manipulate by pushing the appropriate emotional buttons, Scottish politicians still use the language of non-civic nationalism. Non-civic/civic and inclusive/exclusive conceptions exist side by side. When considering the language of manifestos the overarching electoral context may privilege democratic and civic conceptions of nationhood but, as this work indicates, the distinction between the non-civic nation and the nation-state's apparatus is not always clear. Therefore, in a Scottish election where the state has administrative remit over aspects of the nation's cultural life, it is perhaps predictable to see cultural, non-civic articulations of national identity and nationhood. Pressures to administer and support language, sport, the countryside, music and art necessarily draw cultural facets of nationalism into the civic arena. As such, one finds manifestations of these non-civic and sometimes exclusive conceptions of nation and national identity in the language of politicians.

While people operate within a civic context, such as elections, they make decisions appropriate for that context. Scots may well have voted for a parliament and continue to vote in elections informed by civic-nationalism. However, their decision is still underpinned by a sense of national place and national belonging, which can never be fully reconciled with purely civic and inclusive ends. Enough Scots felt not just politically but also culturally different enough to desire greater institutional autonomy. In policy terms, the North East of England and Yorkshire and Humberside are similar to Scotland in their centre-left policy preferences, but neither had the political will to deliver even a moderate form of devolution in 2005. What is the difference? It is not just a sense of political difference; it is a sense of cultural difference and national belonging.

The above analysis illustrates the 'taken for granted' aspects of Scotland, concurrent in the electoral discourse of all the main parties of devolved Scottish politics: all the parties draw on non-civic and civic, and inclusive and exclusive forms of nationalism. In this chapter we have disagreed with a strictly inclusive civic representation of Scottish national identity. It is not that the nationalism displayed is ostensibly civic and inclusive or purely non-civic and exclusive, ethnic and tribal. Instead, there is interplay between differing manifestations. There is ample evidence for the civic and inclusive nationalism, but there are also significantly exclusive and cultural expressions. In politicians' language these, however, are never the fully fledged 'hot' (Billig 1995) and irrational forms that are said to be at odds with democracies. Exclusive and cultural conceptions appear, often innocuously, to co-exist with the other forms. A balance is struck between defining the national 'in-group' as bounded and different but also tolerant and pluralistic as a democracy requires.

5

Mass Perceptions of National Identity: Evidence from Survey Data

INTRODUCTION

The previous two chapters were concerned with elite uses of nationalism as seen in election manifestos, demonstrating, through several levels of content and textual analysis, that these commonplace political documents do not present a straightforward civic and pluralistic articulation of nationalism and national identity. These documents speak from the elite of mainstream political parties to the mass electoral audience. But there must be two sides to any politics of nationalism as democratic elites govern only through popular consent and any movement lacking popular support either withers or remains a marginal force, as the various histories of the Scottish Nationalist movements illustrate (for example Hanham 1969; Lynch 2002). Nationalism as a political force gains its strength from the number of adherents and nationalist identifiers. Bond and Rosie, looking at the constituent national parts of the UK, state that 'identity is an important source of legitimacy for the new political institutions in the UK' (Bond and Rosie 2010: 87). Similarly, Leith has argued that 'a sense of nation and national identity is important to individuals within Scotland' and 'the nation, as portrayed by the political system, serves to connect individuals to a sense of national identity for political purposes' (Leith 2010: 298–9). We have shown that, whatever the political hue of Scottish parties, unionists and Nationalists alike frame many of their policies in the language of national identity. As such, nationalism as a political force in Scottish politics requires an understanding of the content or criteria of national identity within Scotland, at the elite and mass levels, and, of course, of whether there is a correspondence between the two.

Cohen maintains that 'nationalist rhetoric runs a serious risk if it departs from the terms in which individuals can associate themselves with the nation' (Cohen 1996: 810). Cohen's statement addresses the core problem that all political actors, especially the main parties, face in Scottish politics. They must present a sense of the nation and a sense of belonging that appeals to the individuals who constitute it. Politicians within Scotland, whether unionist or Nationalist, project a sense of Scotland that attempts to appeal to all people. Any activity on their part must ensure a connection between the masses and the political elite that both informs, and is informed by, a sense of identity that the masses can identify with as individuals and recognise as a group, or as Rogers Smith puts it, 'leaders' choices are always to some degree restricted by what their potential constituents will accept' (R. Smith 2003: 34).

The ongoing collection of mass data and analysis within Scotland has extended in scope and size in the years since devolution. The British Social Attitudes Survey was well into its second decade of collection when the more specific Scottish Social Attitudes Surveys began. Previous analysis of the data has provided a rich seam for social scientists to mine, particularly in the modernist tradition. The survey data catalogues the attitudes and behaviour of the Scottish electorate and how these interacted with na-tionalism and national identity. In this chapter, we will re-evaluate this survey data to outline how individuals, when aggregated, conceive of their national identity and what criteria of national membership they impose to determine who can, and cannot, be a member of the Scottish nation. The task of this chapter, therefore, is to look at the dynamics of national identity in relation to the constitutional, political and wider cultural inflections, as deducible from the mass survey data.

The analysis begins with a reflection on the strength of feeling as regards a Scottish versus a British sense of identity, shifting then to a consideration of certain key questions relating to the nature of national identity within Scotland. The chapter will continue to an analysis of the interaction between strength of national identification and how individuals construe national belonging and Scottish identity. However, before considering such material, it is necessary to revisit the theoretical divide that challenges any study into nationalism and national identity both within Scotland and upon the wider stage.

Scottish or British? Mass Conceptions of Scottish Nationality

We have already noted the challenges to studying national identity in a sub-state nation like Scotland, not least accounting for the distinction between the sub-state, what we have called the national level, and the state level. Therefore, the first thing to look at is at the distinctions that Scots draw between their national and state identities. During the 1980s the Spanish political scientist Luis Moreno began regular measurement of the nature of national identity within Scotland, and other sub-state national areas. Built on a premise that there may be more than one possible identity in existence at the level of nation and state, the Moreno question has since become well established as part of empirical study into the nature of national identity, enabling a distinction to be drawn between identities and values to be ascribed to those identities. The question therefore establishes a numerical measurement to describe the relationship between identities within a given nation-state, as in the case of the UK where Scottish respondents can express a preference for either Scottish or British identity or a balance between the two. In the UK and Scottish context, results built around the Moreno question have indicated that while the number of those individuals who identify with their Scottish (national) identity over their British (state) identity has increased, this must be treated with some reserve (for a fuller consideration of this and related issues, see McCrone 2001; Brown et al. 1999; and Bond and Rosie 2002). The results in Table 5.1 demonstrate a stable continuum during the immediate contemporary period.

Table 5.1 National identity in Scotland 1997 to 2006 (% by column)

	1997	2003	2006
Scottish not British	32	31	38
More Scottish than British	32	34	35
Equally Scottish and British	28	22	21
More British than Scottish	3	4	2
British not Scottish	3	4	1
Other/none	2	5	–
Base	676	1,508	1,286

Sources: National Election Study 1997, Scottish Social Attitudes Survey 2003, British and Scottish Social Attitudes Survey 2006

From the devolution referendum year of 1997 through to 2006, just prior to the Scottish Parliament's first Nationalist Government, the relationship between the identities changed little. How individuals within Scotland balance being Scottish with British (or not) did not shift dramatically during the nine years between these surveys. The majority of individuals within

Scotland prioritise their Scottishness over being British, while, simultaneously, a majority of individuals within Scotland remain attached to their Britishness, to a greater or lesser degree. Such results provide political manna for individuals and parties on both sides of the Nationalist–unionist divide in Scotland, but provide little direct insight into the nature of national identity.

The Moreno question was not formulated until the 1980s and so no direct comparison with 1979 is possible. However, the issue of questioning an individual respondent on their national identity is not new, and some measurements are available from that period. Mass surveys undertaken in Scotland have regularly contained such questions, and these provide for a comparison in this instance. However, unlike Moreno these questions force respondents to choose between potential identities. Table 5.2 is largely a reproduction of data presented in Bond and Rosie (2002) and cites a number of surveys: Scottish Election Surveys (1974, 1979, 1992 and 1997), the Scottish Referendum Survey (1997), the Scottish Parliamentary Election Survey (1999) and the Scottish Social Attitudes Survey (2000 and 2001). We have computed the final two columns based on the 2003 and 2006 Scottish Social Attitudes Surveys.

Table 5.2 Which nationality best describes you? (% by column)

	1974	1979	1992	1997	1999	2000	2001	2003	2006
Scottish	65	56	72	72	77	80	77	67	78
British	31	38	25	20	17	13	16	25	14
Other/none	4	6	3	8	6	7	7	8	8
Base	588	658	957	882	1,482	1,663	1,605	1,508	1,594

Allowing for certain qualifications at specific political moments in time, the table denotes the pattern of national identifiers since the mid 1970s. The somewhat anomalous results are present in the 1979 and mid to late 1990s figures. The lowest recorded level of Scottish identity in 1979 may reflect the dissatisfaction with the referendum activity of that year. Likewise, the increased numbers of individuals choosing Scottish over British identity in the mid to late 1990s is congruent with the referendum and devolution period. We can also note a decline in the number of Scottish identifiers during the early years of the twenty-first century, indicating that any devolution effect may be waning; however, the rise in British identifiers has not seen a return to 1970s levels. More broadly, the figures indicate a pattern of strengthening Scottishness, allied with a weakening of British-ness over the past three decades.

Adding a party political dimension to the analysis of Scottish national identity results in even greater complexity. Table 5.3 illustrates the lack of a straightforward correlation between support for unionist and Nationalist parties and identification with Britishness and Scottishness respectively.

Table 5.3 National identity and party political support (% by column)

	Lab	SNP	Con	Lib Dem	None	All
Scottish not British	51	65	32	33	58	51
Scottish and British	38	29	38	44	25	33
British not Scottish	8	3	25	18	6	10
N	529	270	206	142	214	1588

Source: Scottish Social Attitudes Survey 2006

A majority of supporters of the unionist Labour Party identify themselves as exclusively Scottish, while nearly a third of SNP supporters maintain Britishness as part of their national identity. Somewhat surprisingly, 32 per cent of Conservatives, the party most identified with England and the Union (McCrone 2001), profess to be exclusively Scottish and not British. Among the non-politically affiliated respondents, a clear majority of 58 per cent consider themselves Scottish and not British, but this does not necessarily transform into automatic support for the SNP. Bond and Rosie's recent analysis showed that 'Being more right-wing has a consistently negative relationship with support for independence' and, contrastively, 'identifying with the SNP has a strongly positive relationship with support for independence', but while 'national identities are significant . . . a degree of "non-alignment" with political attitudes remains evident' (Bond and Rosie 2010: 96). Therefore, in Scotland, support for unionist and nationalist parties or left–right policy preferences are not a reliable guide to an individual's Scottish and/or British identity.

Given that political parties tend to be 'broad churches', with any individual's support likely to be dependent on more than one issue, isolating constitutional preferences with regard to devolution may better serve as markers of national identity. However, as with party political affiliation, this is not the case.

Table 5.4 National identities and constitutional preferences in
Scotland 2006 (% by column)

	Scottish not British	Scottish and British	British not Scottish	All
Scottish independence	42	20	15	30
Devolution status quo	45	65	60	54
No Scottish Parliament	5	12	23	9
N	798	522	178	1,588

Source: Scottish Social Attitudes Survey 2006

In Table 5.4 (quoted from Bond 2009) only around a third of the total respondents support independence, with nearly two-thirds in support of the status quo in the current devolution arrangements or removal of the Scottish Parliament. From the group of respondents who identified themselves as 'only Scottish', 42 per cent were in support of independence and half supported unionist arrangements. Even among those of a British-only identity, 15 per cent are in favour of constitutional separation from the UK; and of those who maintain a dual identity there are 20 per cent in support of independence. Bond (2009: 101) noted, in a comparison with England, that 'what might be termed the "alignment" of national identities and constitutional preferences is certainly stronger than it is in England, but . . . it is hardly strong'.

Putting party political and constitutional preferences together, we can say that those who support the SNP are more likely to profess a Scottish-only identity and support for independence. However, maintaining the current constitutional arrangements as they are is the dominant view across the three identity types, and as Bond concludes:

> But evidence of non-alignment is also extensive, not least with respect to the large proportions of people with an exclusively British identity who show high levels of support for Scottish institutions and those respondents who do not profess any British identity but who nevertheless do not favour constitutional changes or parties which would divide Scotland from Britain politically. (2009: 117)

Therefore, as an earlier study points out, 'only quite a small minority even of "exclusive" Scots support both independence and the SNP, and a much larger proportion of these people in fact support neither' (Bond and Rosie

2002: 43). Looking back the other way, from politics to identity, the time since devolution has not seen a weakening of Scottish identity, but neither has it seen an upsurge of support for independence. Many individuals who feel 'Scottish' do not translate this into support for the SNP whilst many voters who do not support independence for Scotland do support the SNP. Bechhofer and McCrone contend that 'there is no simple connection between national identity and how individuals perceive politics' (Bechhofer and McCrone 2009a: 64) and 'few people see "political" identity as necessary and sufficient for being a Scot' (Bechhofer and McCrone 2009a: 90).

While this data serves to highlight important aspects of national identity within the political arena, it provides no insight into the social and cultural boundaries of national identity. We have shown that all mainstream political parties, particularly in their manifestos, project a mixed sense of national identity, which at one and the same time can be inclusive, modern, forward-looking and distinctly civic in nature, and simultaneously draws on claims of historic and cultural uniqueness, discursively deployed as both bounded and exclusive as well as inclusive and pluralistic, depending on the rhetorical need. As yet we have not addressed how the masses conceive of the nation. It is necessary to understand how individuals within Scotland envisage the criteria of national belonging at a mass level. Is the nation from below similar in vision to that from above? Is the nation of Scotland, according to the people within it, a forward-looking, modern, inclusive nation?

CRITERIA OF NATIONAL BELONGING

It has been asserted that 'there is for the moment no systematic political agenda for exclusion and inclusion in terms of race and ethnicity in Scotland' (McCrone 2001: 173). However, away from the survey data it could be argued that in the 1990s there was a clear political agenda regarding race and ethnicity in Scotland, an agenda that continues today. Our analysis of the major party manifestos highlighted examples of an inclusive sense to both race and ethnicity. This was not limited to any one particular party: few parties provided any firm boundaries that delineated a distinct national belonging for Scotland. In all cases, most especially that of the SNP, any boundaries of the Scottish nation as a people were drawn in a wide inclusive manner. Overall, the precincts of the Scottish nation established by political parties are defined in order to include, not exclude. To assert the absence of a political agenda in terms of race and ethnicity seems misleading, as an inclusive agenda was (or is) obviously present. For evidence, one need look no further than the 'One Scotland Many Cultures' campaign, undertaken by the Scottish Executive in 2002 and continued under the Scottish Government. In November 2009, the Minister for Housing and Communities, Alex Neil, MSP, stated:

> Scotland is a nation of many cultures and beliefs; we have a reputation for being a rich and vibrant place to live, work and visit. However, even today, sadly, racism still occurs and lets us down as a nation. That's why the Scottish Government has developed a new phase of activity under the award winning One Scotland anti-racism campaign . . . We must stand together as One Scotland to tackle the challenges which we face as a nation, only by working together can we all prosper in an equal modern Scotland. (Scotland Against Racism 2009)

McCrone accepts that 'there has been no serious debate about who can and who cannot be Scottish in the past half century' and as such 'we know relatively little about the criteria for Scottish identity, given its long historical pedigree' (McCrone 2001: 172). The survey data, however, does allow for analysis of public opinion in these areas and this data seems to sit at odds with aspects of the modernists' and party political civic and inclusive vision of national identity. To that end these less inclusive versions of nationalism were somewhat discounted, rather than integrated into the description of Scottish national identity, until very recently (see, for example, Bechhofer and McCrone 2009a and b; Bond et al. 2010; and McCrone and Bechhofer 2010).

First, we can start by looking at how criteria for Scottishness and citizenship were answered in a number of different surveys, and how those answers have been portrayed.

Table 5.5 Criteria for Scottishness (% by column)

Response	Birth	Ancestry	Residence
Very important	48	36	30
Fairly important	34	37	35
Not very important	14	22	23
Not at all important	3	4	10
N	882	882	882

Question: 'How important or unimportant is each of the following to being truly Scottish?'

Source: Scottish Election Study 1997: quoted in McCrone 2001

Early in the new millennium, McCrone (2001) argued that the data indicates that while birth and ancestry are important, residence is also accepted as a criterion for Scottishness. Additional support for this point is drawn from the question on the criteria for Scottish citizenship. The question illustrated focused on who would be considered a citizen of Scotland if Scotland were an independent nation. McCrone asserts that, with 52 per cent (see Table 5.6) of respondents seeing residence as an acceptable criterion for citizenship, this 'would make Scotland one of the most open societies in Western Europe in terms of citizenship' (McCrone 2001: 172).

Table 5.6 Criteria for Scottish citizenship

Criterion	% agreeing
Born in Scotland and currently living in Scotland	97
Born in Scotland but not currently living in Scotland	79
Not born in Scotland but currently living in Scotland	52
Not born in Scotland, not living in Scotland, but having at least one parent born in Scotland	34
Not born in Scotland, not living in Scotland, but with at least one grandparent born in Scotland	16
N	1,482

Question: 'Say Scotland did become independent, which of the following kinds of people do you think should be entitled to a Scottish passport?'

Source: Scottish Parliamentary Election Survey 1999

The first of the issues we raise in response is the format of the questions as presented to respondents in the 1999 Scottish Parliamentary Election Study. It is perhaps unfortunate that the framing of the question leaves much unsaid and thus assumed. Each of the responses provides for a hypothetical birthplace of Scotland/Not Scotland, and Not Scotland provides for a large amount of ambiguity. Did respondents assume British-ness on the part of those not born in Scotland? A firmer delineation on this point would provide much clearer and more concise data for consideration and allow greater insight into the perception of national identity and belonging in Scotland.

The second issue to be considered is the response levels themselves and a comparison of the two questions discussed by McCrone and employed as evidence to support his conclusions. Commenting on 1997 data, he states that 82 per cent of people living in Scotland consider birth to be an important criterion for being Scottish; 73 per cent see ancestry (defined as parental and grandparental Scottish birth) as important; and 65 per cent consider residence an important factor. In 1999, similar answers were provided; however, the responses are to a slightly different question. The difference is not merely an artificial one; it does not necessarily follow that the criteria for 'being Scottish' are the same for entitlement to citizenship. The framework shifts from that of asking about Scottishness, an amorphous concept, to that of citizenship, a more clearly defined, institutionally based concept. Responses to the 1999 citizenship question are perhaps less ambiguous than those from 1997, and they also allow for a firmer distinction on grounds of birth, residence and ancestry. For individuals born and living in Scotland 97 per cent of respondents would allow for their entitlement to a Scottish passport; for individuals born in Scotland but not currently living there the positive response declines to 79 per cent. Therefore the difference of 18 per cent amounts to a significant proportion of respondents denying citizenship to non-resident, Scots-born individuals. What remains unclear is whether they would deny non-residents membership of the nation. In both cases, the vast majority are considered Scottish, not only in an 'ethnic' sense of 'being Scottish' but also in an institutional sense, should Scotland be a state or Scottish passports be issued. Both these responses increased between 1997 and 1999. The support given to citizenship is not for being Scottish by virtue of being in Scotland, but for being Scottish because of birthright.

In the 1999 study, the number of respondents supporting residence as a criterion for citizenship is a majority of 52 per cent. In the switch from a question focusing on criteria of national belonging to entitlement to citizenship, the drop in similar responses is 13 per cent. This leaves McCrone's assertion (of Scotland being one of the most open countries in terms of citizenship) open to question, in that it depends on the question being asked. A majority result remains in the 1999 survey, but it is limited at best, and the result is subject to the concerns raised. In short, these two different questions give national identity a different context, and context matters. When more clearly defined and firmer boundaries are in place, the borders of the nation and state specifically delimited, the result is more restrictive, with birthright considered by the public as substantially more important than residence. Therefore, birth and, to a lesser extent, ancestry are evidently important makers of Scottishness in the public mind.

The 2003 Scottish Social Attitudes Survey posed a similar question with regard to who should be entitled to a Scottish passport; unfortunately, the possible responses were framed in a dissimilar fashion than above. The question was part of a series that focused on whether individuals of various groups could be considered 'truly Scottish'. However, the responses again provided a majority category of residence.

Table 5.7 Who should be entitled to a Scottish passport?

Response	% agreeing
Only people who in your view are truly Scottish	26
Anyone permanently living in Scotland	62
Agree with both statements	5
It depends	4
Don't know/not answered	3
N	1,508

Question: 'Suppose that Scotland became independent. Who do you think should be entitled to a Scottish passport and full Scottish citizenship?'

Source: Scottish Social Attitudes Survey 2003

While we may muse about what is meant by 'truly Scottish', the data does provide an unambiguous result. The majority of respondents support the idea that permanent residence alone entails the right to a passport in an independent Scotland. Thus inclusive civic grounds for passport entitlement are more greatly validated by the data from 2003. However, entitlement to a passport is not the same thing as 'being' Scottish.

At this point, then, an understanding of what is and is not 'truly Scottish' would be helpful. Among the several questions asked with regard to attempting to define this category were the following:

- I'd like you to think of someone who was born in England but now lives permanently in Scotland and said they were Scottish. Do you think most people would consider them to be Scottish?
- And now think of a non-white person living in Scotland who spoke with a Scottish accent and said they were Scottish. Do you think most people would consider them to be Scottish?

These questions were also repeated but with the respondent asked if they themselves would consider such individuals as Scottish, shifting the focus from what the respondents think other people would say to what they are prepared to say themselves. These questions go directly to the issues of race and ethnicity and criteria of inclusion and exclusion in the Scottish nation. Being Scottish or English makes an individual British by default, and the presence of and attitudes towards English people in Scotland have been the subject of study (Watson 2003; Bond et al. 2010). The questions also provide distinct attributes concerning potential members of the nation who exhibit different non-civic and racial characteristics.

Table 5.8 Would consider to be Scottish (% by column)

Response	English (most people)	English (respondent)	Non-white, Scottish accent (most people)	Non-white, Scottish accent (respondent)
Definitely would	5	11	5	23
Probably would	25	33	37	47
Probably would not	50	34	42	19
Definitely would not	18	20	12	9
Don't know/not answered	2	2	3	2
N	1,508	1,508	1,508	1,508

Source: Scottish Social Attitudes Survey 2003

The data in Table 5.8 shows a difference between the individual responses and the individual perception of the probable group response. In both questions, individuals provide a more inclusive view than what they think the overall group (people in Scotland) would. A majority positive response to non-white persons with Scottish accents 'being Scottish' is only achieved with individual perceptions. However, the difference between the individual and supposed group response is so great as to raise additional questions about the veracity of the responses (especially on the individual level) overall. In all other categories, and especially in response to English people permanently resident in Scotland, a majority would not consider them Scottish. These results stand in contrast to the responses on the right to a Scottish passport. Although 62 per cent of respondents think anyone permanently residing in Scotland would be entitled to a Scottish passport, this does not directly map onto the specific categories discussed above.

Indeed, responses to the questions concerning the English are perhaps most illustrative. In both cases a clear majority, at either the individual or the group level, would not consider such persons as being Scottish – despite the survey question making it explicit that the subject considers themselves as Scottish. These responses demonstrate that individuals within Scotland do place boundaries upon the nation that are more restrictive than those placed by political parties and institutions within Scotland. Therefore, it is becoming evident that membership of the nation, as perceived at the mass level, is more restrictive than that provided for within the political and elite rhetoric.

Whatever the question, birth remains an important criterion for belonging to the Scottish nation. As previously discussed, a survey in 1997 found that only 17 per cent did not believe birth to be important as a criterion of Scottishness. The question in 2003 was framed differently, with the emphasis being on whether birth was needed to make an individual 'truly Scottish'. In order to divine whether this was a greater requirement amongst Scottish identifiers, the question on birth was cross-tabulated with whether respondents thought of themselves as Scottish.

Table 5.9 Does a person need to be born in Scotland to be truly Scottish? (by whether respondents think of themselves as Scottish) (% by column)

	Scottish	Not Scottish	Don't know/ not answered
Agree strongly	14	6	25
Agree	40	35	0
Neither agree nor disagree	10	12	0
Disagree	28	35	0
Disagree strongly	7	12	0
Don't know/not answered	1	0	75
N	1,273	231	4

Question: 'And some people have different views about what it takes to be truly Scottish. Some say that as well as living in Scotland, to be truly Scottish you have to be born in Scotland. How much do you agree or disagree with this?'

Source: Scottish Social Attitudes Survey 2003

There is variation between the two groups in Table 5.9. The most obvious difference is with those who agree strongly with the requirement of birth to be 'truly Scottish', with 14 per cent of those who consider themselves Scottish falling into this category. This is more than double the percentage of non-Scottish identifiers who see this as important. The 6 per cent who see birth as important is the smallest category of non-Scottish identifiers who made a decision on this question. However, in terms of agreement, rather than strong agreement, the percentages are similar, although again the Scottish identifiers place a greater emphasis on the need for birth than non-Scottish identifiers. Therefore, Scottish identifiers place a higher value on birth with regard to being 'truly Scottish' than non-Scottish identifiers. Indeed, 54 per cent of this group agree with the statement, compared with just over a third who do not see birth as being important. To be a member of the Scottish nation, according to those who identify themselves as belonging to it, birth plays an important role. However, for those self-identifying non-Scots birth is less important, with a sizeable minority of 41 per cent seeing it as important and 47 per cent who do not. Though the position of non-Scots is a little ambivalent, with no majority in either direction, it can be concluded that birth is less important to those who do not identify with the nation, while members of the national group place firmer boundaries around group membership. This result has recently been affirmed by Bechhofer and McCrone (2009b: 18) who found that those who identify strongly with the nation place a 'higher premium for entry'.

Between 1997 and 2003 there appears to have been an marked shift in the perceived importance of a direct connection through birth: in 1997 only 17 per cent saw birth as unimportant, while in 2003, even among Scottish identifiers, this number more than doubled, and among non-Scottish identifiers it is almost a majority. The shift may be due to ambiguities being removed in the wording of questions. Whatever the reason, it is now the case that a significant number of individuals within Scotland no longer see lack of birth in Scotland as a barrier to membership of the nation; for a majority, however, a Scottish birthplace remains an important signifier for national membership.

More recent data available from 2006 allows us to make the kind of comparison we seek, playing non-civic criteria off against each other, specifically against an individual born in England making claims to be Scottish (data is not available regarding whether non-Englishness would have an effect in this comparison). Ethnicity provides an initial differentiation in acceptance by the national group, with non-whiteness making an individual 5 per cent less likely to be accepted by the national group;

Table 5.10 Non-civic criteria of belonging to the national group
(% by column)

	White	White with Scottish accent	White, Scottish accent and Scottish parents	Non-white	Non-white with Scottish accent	Non-white, Scottish accent and Scottish parents
Definitely would	14	19	37	12	15	26
Probably would	30	39	44	26	35	42
Probably would not	30	24	12	31	26	18
Definitely would not	25	16	6	28	22	11
Don't know/ not answered	1	1	1	3	2	2
Base	1,302	1,302	1,302	1,302	1,302	1,302

Question: 'I'd like you to think of a white person who you know was born in England, but now lives permanently in Scotland. This person says they are Scottish. Would you consider this person to be Scottish?'

Source: Scottish Social Attitudes Survey 2006

however, Englishness alone is a barrier to a majority of Scottish respondents. With the addition of a Scottish accent the table shifts to a small majority of Scots granting national membership. Again, however, there is an ethnic differential of 8 percentage points between white and non-whites, and significant minorities regardless of ethnic background exclude English born from the nation group. Finally, with the addition of Scottish parentage, significant majorities manifest support of an English-born individual's right to claim Scottishness; however, there is now a 13 percentage point difference in favour of white individuals, on 80 per cent acceptance. There is therefore a relatively weak effect on the national group granting membership to the nation of a foreign-born (i.e. English-born) individual on the basis of accent, but parentage creates a much stronger positive response from the national group in accepting an outsider, and non-whiteness creates significantly higher barriers to acceptance.

To be clear again, a cross-party political agenda does exist to ensure that

Scotland is considered an inclusive society, especially with regard to race. In 2004–5 and again in 2006 the Scottish Executive undertook a race-equality review. In 2008 the Nationalist Scottish Government launched its Race Equality Scheme. All these efforts are aimed at challenging racism in Scotland and providing for racial equality. Therefore, comparison with mass opinion is important to consider the issue of being Scottish and not being white and revisit certain questions raised by Table 5.8.

Table 5.11 Does a person need to be white to be truly Scottish?
(by whether respondents think of themselves as Scottish)
(% by column)

	Scottish	Not Scottish	Don't know/ not answered
Agree strongly	4	0	0
Agree	11	10	0
Neither agree nor disagree	14	17	25
Disagree	51	44	0
Disagree strongly	20	29	0
Don't know/not answered	1	1	75
N	1,272	231	4

Question: 'And some say that as well as living in Scotland, to be truly Scottish you have to be white – rather than Black or Asian.'

Source: Scottish Social Attitudes Survey 2003

While there are some in Table 5.10 who would agree with the need for an individual to be white to be Scottish, this view is not shared by the vast majority of individuals, whether they consider themselves Scottish or not. A clear majority reject any link between racial characteristics and national belonging with regard to the Scottish nation. Nonetheless, there is a minority in both groups who do see a link between being Scottish and the need to be white, and this number is higher from those who consider themselves Scottish. No non-Scottish identifiers agreed strongly with the question, against 5 per cent of Scottish respondents who did, with the number of those agreeing being almost equal between the two groups. Again, those who identify themselves as members of the nation place firmer criteria of belonging to that nation than non-national identifiers responding to the question.

There must also be questions raised about the veracity of the responses in

Table 5.10 in light of the information provided in Table 5.8, in which 54 per cent of respondents felt that 'most people' within Scotland would not consider non-white people to be Scottish. Also, when individual responses between Tables 5.8 and 5.10 are taken into account the picture is analogous, as differences between Scottish and non-Scottish identifiers in Table 5.10 are almost identical to the individual responses in Table 5.8. In all cases individuals provide one answer, yet Table 5.8 makes it plain that they would consider 'most people' to hold a different view. Opinion with regard to being Scottish and being non-white is far from unambiguous. Individual responses are significantly different from what respondents think 'most people' would profess. This dissimilarity requires the responses to these questions to be treated with caution and leaves the question of race and national belonging in Scotland uncertain. Nonetheless, while Table 5.10 indicates a lack of criteria based upon racial characteristics, the expected group response from Table 5.8 is less positive.

In order to further illuminate the criteria placed upon national member-ship by the masses, we now return to the question posed about hypothetical Scottish citizenship and thus a Scottish passport, originally addressed in Table 5.7.

Previously we have maintained differentiation between citizenship and national belonging or identity. Connor denotes ethnonationalism as re-dundant, 'coined in response to the general tendency to *misuse* the word nationalism to convey loyalty to the state rather than to one's national group' (2004: 10 original emphasis). The misuse of nation and state, and national identity and citizenship is clear for most Scottish respondents. It may well be that when responding to the question 'Suppose that Scotland became independent. Who do you think should be entitled to a Scottish passport and full Scottish citizenship?' an individual is equating the two, but again ambiguity exists and muddies the results. Being Scottish and holding a Scottish passport are not synonymous but the data collection methods used to produce the results employed here seem to accept them as such. A simple but illuminating point is that Scots already share their UK citizen-ship with members of three other nations. Furthermore, the first two words that face UK citizens on their passport are 'European Union'.

Table 5.11 demonstrates differences between the two groups of respon-dents. A significant minority of 28 per cent would reserve passport entitlement to the 'truly Scottish' while only 11 per cent of non-Scottish would do so. Even for those individuals permanently living in Scotland, the figures provide for a definite differentiation, with a difference of 11 per cent showing the Scottish identifiers as being less inclusive. Nonetheless, a solid majority of both groups accept permanent residence to be sufficient for entitlement to a Scottish passport in the event of Scottish independence. The conflation of nation and state within these questions remains, and so the caveats already discussed persist.

Table 5.12 Who should be entitled to a Scottish passport? (by whether respondents think of themselves as Scottish) (% by column)

	Scottish	Not Scottish	Don't know/ not answered
Truly Scottish	28	11	0
Anyone permanently living in Scotland	60	71	0
Agree with both statements above	5	6	0
It depends	4	9	0
Don't know/not answered	2	4	100
N	1,273	231	5

Source: Scottish Social Attitudes Survey 2003

CONCLUSIONS

We opened this chapter with a call for understanding how the masses conceive the Scottish nation in order to balance elite perspectives, both political and academic. Existing studies of the survey data have indicated not only the existence of a strong sense of Scottishness, but also its resilience and continued strength during the past thirty years. Respondents to surveys have provided clear evidence for the argument that Scots prioritise their Scottish identity over their British identity. At the same time, the mere fact of being Scottish, of considering oneself a member of the Scottish nation, is highly complex and not indicative of any one political position or attitude.

Returning to the same data which has been previously employed to argue for the predominance of a civic and inclusive from of Scottish nationalism, we recommended important caveats to the interpretation of that data, and highlighted results which indicate more bounded and exclusive conceptions of Scottishness. The results of Social Attitudes Surveys from 1997 to 2006 make it plain that firmer boundaries are placed upon the nation by the masses than by the mainstream political parties. The mass conception of Scottish national identity has restrictions that serve to exclude certain groups and individuals from membership of the Scottish nation. This interpretation, unfortunately, is not an uncomplicated one as many of the survey questions do not make straightforward distinctions between national and state belonging. When citizenship is foregrounded in questions inclusion widens. Even so, significant minorities of respondents to all surveys would exclude non-whites from being 'truly Scottish' and a majority at the mass level would not consider English and non-white individuals who labelled themselves Scottish as being so. Additionally, these figures greatly increase when respondents are asked what they think their fellow nationals' opinions would be. Place of birth remains influential to attributing national belonging, and many members of the nation would deny membership to individuals not born into the group. Therefore, some non-civic and exclusive criteria of national belonging seem to be at play here. The figures do differ over time: the 1997 devolution vote may have heightened awareness of inclusive forms of national belonging; nonetheless, by 2003 a majority among those who viewed themselves as Scottish saw birthright as being an essential requirement for membership of the nation.

The Scottish modernists' argument, typified in this chapter by McCrone, that Scottish national identity is civic and open in character still holds. We do not refute those results from the survey data which patently point to civic and pluralistic sentiments; however, those non-civic, more bounded and exclusive conceptions of national identity are also demonstrably evident at the mass level. How these two apparently divergent forms fit together is a question that needs to be addressed. McCrone too seems to be altering his position, as in a recent work, co-authored with Frank Bechhofer, they state:

> National identity in Scotland is an unquestioned fact of birth and upbringing in the main, and most people carry it around with them in a taken-for-granted way. They articulate certain common features of being Scottish. They possess and mobilise shared identity markers such as: birth and upbringing, ancestry and parentage, residence, accent, a sense of commitment and belonging, as well as a set of cultural symbols – sport, humour, landscape and languages. (Bechhofer and McCrone 2009a: 89)

What our discussion indicates is that context matters; as such, in a civic context of entitlement to a passport then more open views are evident, but, as the literature has indicated, there is no easy fit between nationalist sentiment and party political affiliation and, therefore, the civic-political arena alone cannot provide an adequate description of Scottish national identity. Even within the civic arena those non-civic attitudes remain in the data, but as the previous chapter illustrated, the deployment of nationalistic tropes in electoral discourse combines those divergent forms of national identity, even in elite language.

6

Narratives of Identity: Locating National Identity in the Public's Discourse

So far, we have outlined a distinction between elite and mass interpretations of national identity, which produce different visions of the same Scotland. On the basis of the mass opinion data there is evidence to suggest a typology of national belonging which places defined non-civic criteria on national membership, including ethnicity, accent, birth and ancestry. The survey data, therefore, agreed with the observations of our manifesto analysis whereby examples of open and pluralistic conceptions of Scottishness coexist with more closed and bounded conceptions. These survey results are, of course, an aggregate of public opinion and tell us little about how an individual's nationalism may manifest itself in daily life. Therefore, to examine how members of the nation enact their individual nationalism we now focus on discourses of, to use Anderson's phrase, 'the daily plebiscite'. Enabled by electronic media and the internet, we examine the language of an online public discussion of a newspaper article. In so doing, we begin to understand some of the ways in which nationalism operates as an everyday discursive phenomenon, as well as the variety of idiosyncratic imaginings that individuals enact.

Billig's banal nationalism analytic, exploring how the homeland is 'flagged' daily in the popular print press, is developed upon. The use of narrative in the 'flagging' of national identity is illustrated. Taking narrative out of 'the novel', we draw a more nuanced picture of how national identity can be discursively 'flagged', going beyond simple grammatical deixis, and again demonstrating an absence of civic and pluralistic instantiations of Scottish national identity in the public's discourse.

BEYOND BANAL NATIONAL IDENTITY

Michael Billig and Benedict Anderson's contribution, particularly their description of the nation's discursive qualities, was touched on in the

Introduction. Billig's concept of 'banal' nationalism has been subjected to further analysis within the social science literature, particularly within a Scottish problematic. Several studies have indicated that the manner in which the nation is 'flagged' deictically in the national media varies from Billig's initial observations in pattern and degree of explicitness. For example, MacInnes et al. (2004) and Rosie et al. (2006) observed that the news publications, and consumption thereof, are substantially different in England and Scotland, and that the 'flagging patterns' in these two geographical areas are discernibly different. In Scotland the deixis is predominantly and explicitly Scottish, while in English based papers the deixis is predominantly English but implicitly so. These findings concur with an earlier study by Law (2001), who notes a qualitative difference between the ways in which the two national centres are flagged: while English-centred newspapers flag British nationalism more implicitly, the Scottish-centred press is more semantically explicit in marking Scotland. Subsequent investigations perceive a problem with Billig's initial use of 'Britain' as a concept for his point of departure, the homogeneous unity of which is called into question (see Jones and Desforges 2003; Law 2001; and MacInnes et al. 2004 and 2007). Even Billig (1995) notes the fiction of this homogenisation of a national press but then goes on to treat it as an unproblematic category.

However, a limitation of much of the critique of *Banal Nationalism* is its narrowness, with its continued and singular locus in deictic analysis. The critique does not dispute Billig's method of analysis; in fact, the problem with the critique is that it tends to reduce the study of banal nationalism to a study of deixis and then seeks to go beyond it. This problem is twofold: first, it is an unjust and somewhat narrow reading of Billig to take his investigation of deixis as the only operation of 'forgotten remembrance'; and second, to cite as a shortcoming that *Banal Nationalism*'s analysis does not consider the production and consumption of nationalist meanings is to misinterpret the substance of the 'banal' thesis. To take the first point, Billig's use of deixis was an illustrative investigation; deixis was not intended to be the primary means of forgotten remembrance. In short, subsequent investigations of banal nationalism have tended to produce more detailed deictic analyses. A notable exception to this has been Higgins (2004b), who took in a semantic component to language, looking at what he terms 'location formation' through the use of 'location lexical tokens'.

Regarding the second problem, the critique of Billig often attempts to go beyond the textual condition of deixis to the producers and consumers of texts, which appears a necessary move after undermining the deixis of banal nationalism. If the categories of 'Britain' and the 'national press' are ambiguous or analytically difficult, then it is necessary to go beyond the text and investigate the production and consumption of texts to ask what the makers of the texts meant by their national references and what consumers interpreted them to be. These are entirely reasonable and productive courses of enquiry; they do not, however, amount to an actual critique of the 'banal nationalism' thesis. The critique is an analysis of the 'mindfulness' of production and consumption of the national sign; whereas Billig has under-lined that 'the concern is to notice the unwaved flag, and to decode other cultural artefacts, in order, again, to notice the assumptions of nationhood which are habitually overlooked' (Billig 1997: 488). He goes on:

> The more the phenomenology of consumption (or production) becomes the focus of attention, the more this taken-for-granted locus will be forgotten, but thus forgetting itself is part of the reproduction of the locus. A different analytic perspective – one which does not concentrate on either production or consumption – is necessary. (Billig 1997: 489–90)

An additional difficulty with the critique of Billig is that the studies all focus on the 'national' press as a way of discussing and investigating mass participation in 'homeland making'. Of course, the Scottish media has been cited as one of the main ways in which Scottishness can be enacted publicly (for a recent example see Higgins 2004b: 634). Nevertheless, these approaches present a rather large difficulty: they look at the writings of journalists and conflate them with their reading audiences (MacInnes et al. 2004). The collapsing of writers and readers into each other has been a necessary evil when exploring the discursive aspects of nations and nationalism. However, online editions of newspapers with threads in which readers can post their responses to articles allow an opportunity to investigate reactions of members of the public. These responses need not merely be read as reactions of a readership, but also as loci of nationalist production themselves. We will focus on these readers' responses in the sections below.

NARRATIVE AND NATIONAL IDENTITY

As we have discussed, Billig's initial application of deixis has been reapplied many times, to the point where the analysis itself has become somewhat banal. Semiotically, subsequent studies have done little (with the exception of Higgins 2004a and b) to look at other ways in which the nation is flagged, banally or otherwise. In this chapter we develop deictic analysis, first by integrating deixis into a wider framework of location formation within discourse and second, by using that framework to investigate individuals' narratives of national identity in an authentic example of public discourse (as opposed to semi-structured interviews or focus groups, for relevant examples of which see Bechhofer and McCrone 2009b and Wodak et al. 1999).

Our modification of deictic analysis starts by making a three-way distinction in how deixis marks a text, borrowing Chilton's (2004: 56–62) framework. Chilton proposes three dimensions of deixis, which he calls 'axes': the spatial, temporal and modal dimensions. The spatial axis plots an antithetically distal position relative to the 'here' of an utterance. For example, in 'here in the West we believe in democracy, unlike in the Middle East' deictic expressions 'here', 'in' and 'the West' point to the physically present context, whereas 'in' and 'the Middle East' plot distal points for subjects removed from that physically present context. Similarly, the temporal axis plots points relative to the 'now' of an utterance, where subjects are encoded as either in the past or of the future. These two axes also facilitate the encoding of social deixis, where individuals or groups are plotted and conceptualised as being sometimes temporally, but more often spatially distal from the 'I' or 'we' of the utterance. We follow Chilton in not separating social deixis out from the spatial or temporal axes (though he does note that they usually are) because 'them' or 'you', realised as psychologically distal, implicitly encodes separateness from 'I' or 'we'. This is to underline a more general point about all the deictic axes: they are all linguistically realised through spatial metaphors (Lakoff and Johnson 1980). The third axis of 'modality' plots relative positions of truth and rightness. This dimension is connected to morality and ideology and is conceptualised in terms of proximity to the deictic centre. Expressing rightness and trueness in terms of physical location is borne out by familiar expressions: 'he is *way out* in left field on this issue', 'you are a *long way off* the mark' and 'the parties are *far* from reaching an agreement'. Therefore, the morality of 'rightness' and 'trueness', in ideological terms, is expressed as spatial proximity to the utterer/writer, whereas antithetical positions appear as relative degrees of distance from that point. Modal verbs are most typically cited (Simpson 1993) to represent modalities of 'rightness' and 'trueness', for example should/shouldn't, will/won't, can/can't and must/mustn't. Nouns, verbs and adjectives (or paralinguistic features like intonation in spoken discourse) may also perform the same function, for example 'good/evil', 'honest/dishonest', which are antonymic values and therefore represent cognitively separate positions.

Those who create discourses and those who receive and process them will mentally 'locate arguments and predicates by reference to points on the three axes *s*, *t* and *m*' (Chilton 2004: 60–1), as in Figure 6.1, which are flagged by textual features of the discourse. Coordinates are identified on the three axes and used to navigate and find meaning in the discourse as it progresses. This model goes beyond the traditional definition of deictic 'closed-class' words (prepositions, modal auxiliary verbs, pronouns and articles); it also includes 'open-class' words (nouns, verbs and adjectives) that still perform a similar pointing or anchoring function, which can be plotted on the same axes. The difference between traditional deixis and our expanded sense could be summed up by the distinction between the closed-class word 'here' and the open-class word 'Scotland', both of which could be used to deictically point to the same space (assuming the speaker is in Scotland). The latter example is similar to what Higgins (2004b) refers to as 'location lexical tokens'. Now, with our initial analytic framework drawn, we can introduce the explanation of why narratives may be a useful site of enquiry.

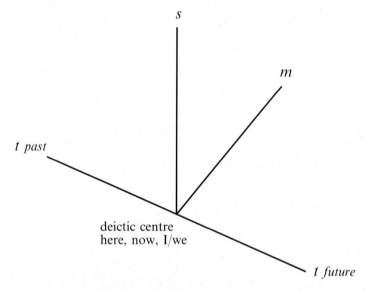

Figure 6.1 Deixis axes (from Chilton 2004: 60)

Through the consumption of print, we all have access to stories of our national selves, whether we are directly involved in the telling or not. 'Awareness of being embedded in secular, serial time, with all its implications of continuity, yet of "forgetting" the experiences of this continuity . . . engenders the need for a narrative identity' (Anderson 2006: 205). Within the complex milieu of the personal and political, one's national identity is necessarily a tool by which we make sense of ourselves in the modern state, drawing boundaries and defining relationships of wider association and then justifying boundaries and associations within discursive events. Justification can come in the form of stories of why things are the way they are, how we got here and what that means to us. Rogers Smith has begun to lay foundations for political scientists to build on, marking out some theoretical territory for investigating the narratives that are used to support political and, more particularly, national movements. He comments that 'stories of peoplehood do not merely serve interests, they also help to constitute them, for aspiring leaders and potential constituents alike' (R. Smith 2003: 45). Narratives are salient in relation to discourse because they are an author's interpretation of the meaning of a series of connected agents, events and places. At a more ideological level:

> narratives of peoplehood work essentially as persuasive historical stories that prompt people to embrace the valorized identities, play the stirring roles, and have the fulfilling experiences that political leaders strive to evoke for them, whether through arguments, rhetoric, symbols, or 'stories' of a more obvious and familiar sort. (R. Smith 2003: 43)

The narratives we look at are not only those of epics and printed novels, which Anderson considered, or those of Smith's (2003) political elites; instead, they are everyday and 'banal' in character, the type of stories we all might tell about ourselves. We begin, therefore, to see how the nation is woven into the meaning of our lives, how people interpret themselves in relation to their nation, and the different kinds of nation, and people, at play in this telling.

First, how should what is and what is not a narrative be determined, amongst the many possible discursive structures? According to Lamarque, 'In the most general terms, to narrate is to tell a story . . . Narration of any kind involves the recounting and shaping of events.' Lamarque continues, 'A mere catalogue of descriptive sentences does not make a narrative. For one thing there must be *events* described, not just things' (Lamarque 1990: 131, original emphasis). Therefore, narratives entail things happening and involve agents carrying out actions or being subject to them; a shopping list, therefore, is not a narrative. But even a list of actions to be carried out does not count as narrative. For example, consider a fictional academic's 'To Do' list which could be sitting on her desk as she types: write chapter for two hours; phone Professor Marx; check student workshop sign-ups; email the Mitchell Library. Even though this list contains the verbs 'write', 'check', 'phone' and 'email', so a reader can deduce that certain things are to be done or have been done and other 'things' have or will be acted upon, a reader would be making a rather large interpretive leap to relate these separate actions and events together into a meaningful story. This is because a narrative orders and implies meaningful relations between its constituent parts. Additionally, things are made meaningful partly because 'for every narrative there is a narrator, real or implied or both. Stories don't just exist, they are told, and not just told but told from some perspective or other.' (Lamarque 1990: 131)

Therein lies the rub: it is not the happening of events but the telling of them that is significant for narratives. A telling from a particular point of view engenders a need for a means of mapping positions in the discourse. The relationship between the story and its teller is an important one because it opens up textual dimensions for analysis. For example, on one plane there is a narrative consisting of a series of events, perhaps with one or more characters, which occurs over a certain timespan, all of which we can identify and describe. On another plane, we must consider the position assumed by the narrator in their narration; most simply, a comparison should be made between those narrators involved in the story they are telling and those who assume an external stance. Already this additional dimension in the focus of analysis increases the level of complexity. The interaction between the two planes may be significant, for example, in determining whether a narrator claims a subjective or objective perspective. If deictic markers are drawn on here, the use of pronouns such as 'I' or 'we' or locations of space such as 'here' or 'there' position a narrator in relation to the events being told and tell us something about the type of narrator they are and how they are situating themselves and their story in relation to their readers. If the narrator is absent, with no 'I/me/my', then references to themselves may indicate an 'objective' stance in relation to their subject matter and a resulting authoritative tone. The use of 'I/me/my' places the narrator in a subjective position within their story and so more personal perspectives are likely to ensue. It is not possible to say definitively why people write the narratives they do, and that is not the point of this type of analysis. Rather, we are further exploring the discursive resources members of the national community have at their disposal and how they deploy them. Through looking at narratives, we can illustrate the dynamism of Scottish nationalist reference and show how the nation is flagged in sets of competing and sometimes mixed narratives, in which it is positioned in relation to varying constructions of the individual and collective self, spatial and temporal continuities, and ideological stances. We break our analysis into three main narrative types prevalent in the online discussion: historical, personal and ideological. This typology reflects the character of the narratives told. Historical narratives relate stories from the past, personal narratives draw on the individual narrator's experience and ideological narratives are told in support of some political and in this instance, nationalist, position.

ONLINE DISCUSSION THREADS

The online discussion thread follows on from the online publication of the 'Painting of Forgotten Warrior Unveiled' article also published in the print form of the *Herald* newspaper on 23 October 2007. The discussion threads allowed readers to post responses to the article; these responses vary from the very short to more lengthy, polemical contributions. Although the contributions are subject to monitoring there is a great deal of room for freedom of expression, as statements like 'those English boot-lickers called "London Labour"' and 'it's the descendants of this clown and Bruce who sold you for English gold' suggest. Contributors are indicated by their username, which may be a proper name, a nickname or an assemblage of letters and numbers. Some contributors make only a single post, while others make multiple postings which engage with other contributors' comments. There is therefore an element of public discussion and inter-action in the threads which makes them an apposite place to investigate wider public discourse of items present in the media. Online contributors may not be prototypical readers and may represent a particularly 'enthu-siastic' readership. However, our interest in these threads is not to represent reader responses in general, but to use them as an example of wider public discussions of nationalism and the nation which are 'out there' and readily available. In our sample, a broad spectrum of opinions is evident, from moderate to extreme, from intensely engaged to whimsical or facetious.

Our sample is approximately 5,000 words in length and includes the first 40 posts, recorded chronologically on the *Herald*'s website after the posting of the associated article. Contributors' names have been changed for anonymity, though where necessary for semantic continuity we have changed a contributor's username to a pseudonym similar in meaning.

ANALYSIS: PAINTING OF FORGOTTEN WARRIOR UNVEILED

Below is a condensed version of the article, detailing the unveiling of a modern painting of a medieval Scottish knight, the Black Douglas:

> A painting of a forgotten Scottish medieval warrior has been unveiled by his descendants determined that his place in history should be recognised . . . The Duke and Duchess of Hamilton, together with the Marquis of Douglas and Clydesdale and Lord Selkirk of Douglas, unveiled the picture at Lennoxlove House . . . the family said as a companion of William Wallace and Robert the Bruce the Black Douglas was instru-mental in the fight for independence from the English in the 14th century. (Donnelly, *Herald*, 23 October 2007)

The subsequent online discussion initially concerns itself with further historical details of the Black Douglas, as well as picking up on the article's presupposition that he is a 'forgotten' Scottish icon. Further posts reflect not just on the article but also on the other online comments themselves, concurring with and disputing the points being made. As such, the discussion is not only of the painting of the Black Douglas but also more broadly of nationalistic issues too: authentic national heroes, nationalist-unionist arguments, the nature of national history taught in schools and Scotland's role in the British Empire. This particular article suits our purposes because it is not specifically about nationalist issues, yet it provokes online debate permeated with representations of the nation and national identity. Illustrated below are a number of narrative strategies, that is ways of telling stories, employed therein.

Historical narratives

These are representations of the nation through the recounting of narratives focused on events, places, people and things in past time. The following was the second post made, contributed by 'Duncan of Glasgow', and provides additional historical commentary on the life of the Black Douglas. Key to our discussion is the manner in which the text locates Scotland in a number of ways, particularly as a piece of narrative story-telling.

> [Posted by: Duncan, Glasgow at 4:59am]
> His family motto, of a heart, is the real Braveheart and his full swashbuckling story would make a real sweep of a film. He recaptured his castle with only one other person, by climbing up the walls, grabbing a guard by the throat and dispatching the whole garrison in the night and chopping their bodies into pieces in the flour, wine and other provisions before retreating. This tactic became known as the 'Douglas Larder' and was used by Wallace and the Scottish Guerrilla army too. He was a master of hit and run tactic against superior odds, used also by the Bruce and the Scottish army, with their raids into England and their garrisons in Ireland. His Statue in Portugal, marking where he fell, was typical of Scots impetuosity. The Scots charged the Saracens, whilst the Spanish King held back. His body was recovered with Bruce's heart around his neck, in a circle of Saracen bodies.

Although Scotland as a geographical place or nation is not directly referenced, the narrative locates Scotland in a number of different ways which correspond to the axis outline above. The narrator assumes a detached position external to the narrative. There are no personal 'I' or 'we' referents; rather, the narrator presumes to tell a story about the Black Douglas, situating it within the 'real' of actual historical events, grammatically constructed with categorical statements. Therefore, the most obvious location to start with is the temporal.

This is an historical narrative, with the tense of the 'swashbuckling' Black Douglas located in the past, as in 'He *recaptured* his castle', 'The Scots *charged* the Saracens'. However, the narrator starts his narrative in the present tense, as if with a prologue tacitly linking to the original article by reference to the Black Douglas pronominally as a given 'His', and eulogising the Douglas family motto 'of a heart' as 'the real Braveheart'. This connects the following narrative to 'our' present. The narrative then transitions to a series of connected actions carried out by the Black Douglas as he recaptures a castle and chops up some English bodies to be fed to an unsuspecting 'auld enemy'. These actions begin in the past tense ('He *recaptured* his castle') before transitioning to the present continuous of '*grabbing* a guard by the throat and *dispatching* a whole garrison'. Then there is a switch back to the past tense, as the narrator omnisciently comments categorically as a detached observer, 'This tactic *became known* as the "Douglas Larder" '.

Continuity between the spatial and temporal locating of Scotland in the narrative is evident. It is about a Scot who 'is the real *Braveheart*', flagging that most contemporary cinematic cliché of Scottish nationalism, and we are also told that the Black Douglas's heroic death was 'typical of *Scots* impetuosity'. Other spatial references are given, including 'their raids *into England*', as well as other nouns marking the geographical areas of 'Ireland' and 'Portugal' as places antonymic or at least differentiated unproblematically from medieval Scotland. Therefore, the spatial continuity of Scotland is coterminous with its temporal continuity from the past to our reading in the present.

Though a detached narrative position is assumed by the post's author, Scotland is located positively on the modal axis, as we are told the Black Douglas's story 'would make a *real* sweep of a film', that his family motto 'is the real Braveheart' and that the manner of his death 'was *typical* of Scots impetuosity'. The two uses of 'real' are emphatic claims to authenticity, whereas 'typical' and 'impetuosity' positively evaluate the Black Douglas's action and death in heroic terms, placing this Scottish icon close to the writer's modal centre. Therefore, in this instance the historical roots of the nation are being dug up from ancient historical soil. The characterisation of this particularly Scottish narrative is distinctly non-civic, historical and tribalistic.

A second example of an historical narrative repeats this pattern of location, though the narrative is even shorter:

[Posted by: Damien Kirk, Edinburgh at 9:35am]
'Guid Sir James' is a true Scottish hero and was also well respected in Europe as a highly rated knight of Christendom.

Of course he indulged in a bit of limb chopping, but what self respecting medieval warrior wouldnt [sic]?

Taking Bruce's heart on crusade was a great mvoe [sic] and although he didnt [sic] succeed, he died gloriously in trying . . . you can't get better than that!

The only thing about this article is that it says 'forgotten hero' . . . is he? Not by me he isnt [sic] . . . if he is then it is a sad sign of our times.

Again, the structure of the narrative starts with an authoritative detached narrator informing readers of the Black Douglas's historical reputation, beginning an evaluative framing: ' "Guid Sir James" is a *true Scottish hero* and was *respected* in Europe as a *highly rated* knight of Christendom'. Here the text is immediately located on a number of axes. The past tense evokes past time, as do the nouns 'knight' and 'Christendom', which embody temporal and spatial connotations both of which are evocative of medieval Europe; more specifically, 'Scottish hero' gives further locative exactness. In the first sentence the narrative is positioned modally too, with the adjective 'true', the positive noun 'hero' and the adverb-participle combinations 'well respected' and 'highly rated' situating the Black Douglas, as 'true Scottish hero', modally proximate to a reading Scottish audience.

The narrative then moves on to Sir James's military actions, once more in the historical past, indicated by tense and the adjective 'medieval'; this second sentence, however, is also posed as a rhetorical question of 'what self respecting medieval warrior wouldnt [sic]'. This acknowledges a subjectivity of historical actions and, as such, implicitly references several earlier posts that questioned the eulogising of violent historical figures and a straightforward and unproblematic reading of history. The narrative moves on to Sir James: 'Taking Bruce's heart on crusade' is valorised modally as a '*great move*', and even though he never made it to the Holy Land he '*died gloriously*', to which our narrator comments, 'you can't get better than that!' Here we have a short sequence of historical events (going on crusade and then dying) temporally located distally in the past, but modally located close to our narrator. The final sentence then transitions out of the narrative storytelling to comment on the original article and back into the present tense to deny the validity of the article's assertion that Sir James is a 'forgotten hero'. Now the narrator appears pronominally to proclaim 'Not by *me* he isn't' and then inclusively references the national reading collective with the 'sad sign of *our* times'.

The number of ways in which the nation is located is evident, so that a national deixis is not just a question of flagging 'us' 'here' and 'now'; those three deictic markers – social, spatial and temporal – do not exist on a one-dimensional point where 'we', inhabiting 'this' space at 'this' time, coalesce. Instead, those associations engender further continuities across time, utilising diverse markers which may stand for the social 'us' and evoke differing visions of 'this' national space. National references do not exist in a textual vacuum; they are employed within different and perhaps competing rhetorical strategies. Discursively, the material drawn on in these historical narratives is exceptionally atavistic and non-civic in substance.

Personal narratives

Another narrative strategy used is what we term 'personal narratives'. They are 'personal' because of the manner in which narrators utilised stories from their own lives in response to the *Herald*'s article and other online posts, these narratives make connections between narrators, their childhood, historical events and the nation. The multiple axes of location allow us to see the nuanced ways in which authors constituted the nation in narrative. In this next example the narrator intertwines the historical and the personal.

> [Posted by: Pat2000, Dunfermline at 6:41am]
> My old Aberdeenshire County Council primary school history book in the fifties had a thick chapter on the Wars of Independence which I read a thousand times. It told the tales of Bruce, Wallace, the Black Douglas (my favourite) and the Red Randolph. The last page was a quick few lines on the Union of the Crowns and Parliaments and that was it! End of story. Can we not get that book back in print and back into the kids [sic] hands? Why was it ever shelved? I do not know but I can guess.

The use of the pronouns 'I' and 'my' immediately places the narrator in the narrative, which is coterminous with one of the two temporal pasts being constituted. The first of these is the narrator's childhood with 'My *old* Aberdeenshire . . . primary school', 'in the *fifties*' and 'I *read* a thousand times'. This past is connected to the narrator by deictically flagged personal pronouns. The second past is the subject of history itself, as in 'tales of Bruce, Wallace and the Black Douglas' and 'the Union of the Crowns and Parliaments'. Those two temporal lines also share the same spatial location, indicated by the nouns marking a contentious Scottish relation with England, with 'Aberdeenshire' denoting place and 'the Union of the

Crowns and Parliaments' inferring both a temporal and spatial specificity. Narratively, the text is a story within a story, a childhood reminiscence of historical narratives enjoyed at school, which, in the narrator's opinion, gave the proper weight to historical events, dwelling only briefly on 1603 and 1707 ('End of story'). If the ideological motivation behind the narrative is too opaque for readers, the narrator poses his own rhetorical questions and answers them as well. In the first question, the personal reference widens to the social, as the collective 'we' is invoked and 'the kids' mentioned are inferentially 'our' kids. Rhetorically speaking, the personal aspects of the narrative are utilised as a basis for a preferred non-English, non-British reading of Scottish history. The identity of the history book in question is ambiguous; later posts clarify the book's identity and take up the ideological vein of this narrator's contribution.

Contrastively, a second type of personal narrative observed utilises personal references in a very different manner. In the same way, these narrators are pronominally in their own reminiscences, for example 'I have fond memories of the Corries too – many of their songs (my Granny had all their 8-tracks) constituted a soundtrack to my childhood' or 'I seemed to impress my Primary 3 teacher by being able to spell "Bruce and de Bohun" fairly correctly'. We are anchored initially in both a subjective and an individual perspective of the authors. As readers, we are also temporally located in their childhood pasts, playing while listening to Granny's music or sitting working in a primary school lesson. This type of personal narrative is still placed within a Scottish context, most obviously flagged nominally by 'Scots' but also flagged inferentially with 'the Corries' and 'the Bruce'. These narrators, however, do not rhetorically use their childhood narratives as a pretext for atavistic musings; rather, naive childhood is used contrastively against a more mature adult reading of history – but this is an ambivalent position in relation to nationalism. For example, Duncan Kerr comments:

> my childhood games of 'sojers' and Knights and Castles . . . often had a virtuous Scots Vs. the dastardly English theme. Reading and the growing realisation that contexts transcending 'whas like us?' simplisms meant that I had begun to grow out of that line of think [sic] by, oh . . . age 12'.

The contrastive side of these narratives puts forward an alternative reading, such as:

> While its [sic] understandable, and no doubt good fun, to have rousing, national heroes full of martial virtue (and then some!) who stuck it to the

forces of a stronger, belligerent neighbour, what I find interesting is the extent to which the Black Douglas is being valorised for his exploits in Iberia.

(In this last post 'exploits in Iberia' refers to the Black Douglas and the ring of Saracens' bodies he was found in.)

A similar conclusion is reached in the following post by JAMES.T:

> I've long been troubled by the way we have celebrated some of the most awful things in our history. I don't mean to traduce those who did what they did in the most difficult and trying circumstances of their times, but to relish their chopping people into bits and mixing their flesh, bones and blood, etc. with flour and wine surely is a bit odd?

In both types of personal narratives, the subjective self becomes entwined with 'objective' historical narratives. The two different uses of personal narratives illustrate rhetorical flexibility in achieving different ends: the initial narrator portrays a naive reading of history, with its more clear-cut ideological inferences, while the second two use personal narratives to question 'naive' readings of history as valorisations in the present. However, both types of personal narrative are unable to avoid the implicit context of a Scottish nation; although in the second two personal narratives take no explicit stance towards the nation or nationalism, they are still deictically, that is banally, situated in the national reading context.

Ideological narratives

Ideological narratives are explicitly argumentative in style, mobilised to support a political position. Take, for example, the following short text, which was the fifth posted online:

> [Posted by: tar0001 at 7:58am]
> The book was called 'the Story of Scotland'. All this talk of the Black Douglas should stir the blood of all true Scotsmen. Today the fight [sic] against those English boot-lickers called 'London Labour' who would deny us our freedoms, our culture, disrupt the peace of the world and like Edward I threaten the very existence of Scotland.

This is the shortest of narratives and initially starts as an interlocution following on from a previous post. Historical exploits of the Black Douglas are a rally to nationalist authenticity which 'should stir the blood of all *true*

Scotsmen'. The past is invoked for the purposes of the present and mapped modally proximate by 'true'. Our narrator switches to the present, with a short narrative encapsulating the present 'fight' against the ideologically antithetical 'English boot-lickers called London Labour', which mirrors Scotland's medieval battles with Edward Longshanks. 'England' and 'London' are marked as spatially separate. In addition, those entities are confirmed as modally antonymic to 'Scotland' by the derisory term 'boot-lickers', which plots both England and 'London Labour' as modally distal. This narrative indicates the given Scottish (not British) national collective by the use of social deixis, in this instance 'us' and 'our'. This is not the same as the individualised personal narratives above but rather is a narrative that is collectively situated. Rhetorically, what makes the narrative ideological is the employment of different discursive resources in producing contrasts between discourse participants – 'us' versus 'them' – and the spatial location of those groups as 'here' versus 'there'. As such, it follows that ideological narratives are less ambiguously pro their 'home' nation and anti some other nation(s), but in other online contributions it is not a simple case of being anti-England and pro-Scotland.

The previous example reduces Scottish nationalism to an 'us' Scots versus 'them' English simplism, and it is relatively easy to find other such examples, as we have here. However, other online posts in response to the Black Douglas article evoke a more complex relationship between Scotland and England, not least with the concept of Britishness, but also with reference to Scotland's relationship with other nations. For example, the tone of the posts by 'Battling Irish' has a rather derisory timbre as regards Scotland's relationship with England, provoking much subsequent debate on the website. 'Here we go again. Another patriot who fought for so called Scottish freedom. Another patriot from over 700 years ago!!' begins Battling Irish, continuing with:

> The real irony is it's the desecendants [sic] of this clown and Bruce who sold you for English gold and boy didn't you lot buy in hook, line and sinker. I find it hilarious the comments on here about London Labour subjugating poor wee Scotland.

Again, there is the beginning of a chain of related events and agents of a narrative. 'Here we go again' functions as a sardonic variation of 'once upon a time', discursively signalling the beginning of a narrative. Actions are delimited as 'fought', 'sold' and 'buy in', agents are 'patriot', 'descendants' and the collective national 'you' and 'you lot'; these actions and events, though temporally disparate, are bound together in the continuity of the national collective. The ideological nature of the narrative is indicated by the modally antithetical positions of the positive Irish and the negative Scots/Brits. Continuing in a similar vein, Battling Irish writes:

> If you had any backbone you would have freed yourself years ago. If you had any backbone your sons (as Ireland's did) would have never accepted being ruled by foreigners. Instead for hundreds of years you bought into, contributed to and aided and abetted the biggest criminal organisation that this planet had ever seen . . . yes that's right . . . The British Empire and now you've got the cheek to say that England is subjigating [sic] you. You've allowed these criminals to tie you into their atrocities. You became their lap dog, patrionised [sic] at every turn (how fierce your soldiers are? How good your administrators are? etc etc etc)
>
> What a bunch of snivelling cowards. When everything was going your way and you were lording it over the rest of the planet it was fine. Now when times are tough your [sic] blaming labour for dragging you into illegal wars. What a joke. Your [sic] quoting black douglas from 700 years ago . . . what about what happened in between? crimes against the irish, the Indians, African natives, drug pushing to the Chinese. Go and read about the Pontiac rebellion where you lot inflicted a whole North American tribe with Smallpox through infected blankets!!! Guilty to a man the lot of you. Where were your heroes when all this was going on . . . I'll tell you joining in . . . that's where . . . doing the killing and taking the profit.
>
> Salmond says Scotland can be a new Ireland . . . Dont [sic] see it . . . You lack moral courage! Terrible people . . . Terrible country that divorces itself from its crimes.

It is argumentative and provocative, and gives an impression of the type of posts which the *Herald* permitted to be published on its website at that time (the newspaper has since removed the online threads following articles). Battling Irish's comments are a rebuttal to those who claim a post-colonial subject position for Scotland, emphasising Scotland was a colonial power as part of Britain. The narrative is combined with use of inflammatory language, negatively questioning the particular nationalistic ideological point of view that seeks to separate Scotland from England and the rest of the UK, along with its interpretations of history. It does this, in large part, by retelling another narrative with other historical events as counter examples to the heroic Black Douglas as an authentic paragon of Scottishness. This creates another sense of Scottish identity, one constructed from outside, and links it to other events, times and places.

Battling Irish's narrative shifts temporally between medieval Scotland, the British Empire and the present, using the pronoun 'you' and possessive pronoun 'your' to repeatedly reaffirm the connection between the present national collective and peoples of the past. The narrative begins in the distant past with 'Another patriot *from over 700 years ago*', while the next sentence, '*desecendents* [sic] of this clown and Bruce who *sold* you for English gold and boy *didn't* you lot buy in hook, line and sinker', creates a temporal continuity between actors across time, with 'you' encompassing not just 'you' present Scots but also 'you' historic Scots as well. A series of actions are imputed to Scots and these actions and their agents are syntactically situated in past time, for example with the adverbial phrase 'for hundreds of years' and then with actions in the past tense: 'bought into', 'contributed to', 'aided' and 'abetted'. The narrative moves back to the present with a comment on other posts, 'and *now* you've got the cheek to say that England *is subjugating* [sic] you'. The subsequent paragraph also makes connections between the past (for example, '*When* everything *was going your way*') and the present (for example, '*Now* when times are tough'), with actions put in the present continuous tense, for example, '*blaming*' and '*dragging*', indicating the ongoing nature of the present actions of the 'you' Scots of the present.

A dominant theme of Battling Irish's narrative is that of a collective Scottish national guilt versus heroic Irish exploits, which plots apposing points on the modal axis, with the Irish being modally proximate and the Scots, along with the British and English, modally distal. Discourse markers, which act like discursive signposts, such as 'Here we go again', 'so called', 'The real irony is', 'I find it hilarious', 'If you only had a backbone' and, of course, 'What a bunch of snivelling cowards', produce a sardonic frame for the narrative and contribute to modal distance. The social deictic marker 'you', standing for Scotland and the Scots, is con- sistently associated with negatively evaluated actions, so that '*you became* their lap dog', '*you've allowed* these criminals to tie *you* into their atrocities' and '*you bought into, contributed* to and *aided* and *abetted* the biggest criminal organisation in history'. Grammatically, in these clauses Scotland is an active actor in the performance of negative actions. Clause structures like these have been identified as a strategy in discourse for constructing ideological responsibility for actions (see Simpson 1993: 86–117 and Fowler 1986: 156–62). Contrast these active sentences with Battling Irish's sarcastic comment 'I find it hilarious the comments on here about London Labour subjugating poor wee Scotland', where Scotland, the sentence object, is in a passive position in the clause having the action of the verb done to it and London Labour is the subject, performing the verb on Scotland. This pattern of passivity is inverted by the prefacing comment 'I find it hilarious'. Contrastively, the Irish are denoted in positive terms; the sons of Ireland have 'backbone' and threw off the English yoke whereas those sons of Scotland do not; they accepted foreign rule and actively participated in the atrocities of Empire. Scotland cannot be like heroic Ireland because, according to Battling Irish, it lacks 'moral courage' and is a 'terrible people' divorcing itself 'from its crimes'.

Multiple narrative types

Though we have separated out the types of narrative for descriptive clarity, it is often the case that more than one narrative strategy is used by a writer to achieve their communicative end. The narratives, though frequently brief, are intricate discursive phenomena; for example, several of the personal narratives above utilised stories of personal experience as a rhetorical strategy to present a relativist and contingent view of history. These posts question perspectives and the application of historical events to present nationalistic ideological concerns, but it is not that these posts question the rightness or wrongness of historical actions within their given historical context; rather, they question the valorisation of those actions in the present. They query the legitimacy given to the 'naturalness' of the connections ascribed between the past and the present. We have already looked at JAMES.T's post above, but return to it here to illustrate how narrative is used as an eristic tool.

> [Posted by: JAMES.T, Berkeley at 6:54am]
> I don't mean to traduce those who did what they did in the most difficult and trying circumstances of their times, but to relish their chopping people into bits and mixing their flesh, bones and blood, etc. with flour and wine surely is a bit odd? But maybe it's just because I've just finished reading Alistair Horne's 'A Savage War of Peace', an account of the atrocities committed on all sides in the Algerian War and reflecting that that sort of thing has recurred again and again in my lifetime, that I find myself heartily wishing that the peacemongers got even a fraction of the recognition that the warriors keep on receiving.

JAMES.T begins with a mitigation of the actions of medieval warriors 'who did what they did in the most difficult and trying of circumstances', using a temporal specification 'of their times'. The mitigation, however, is of those figures in history and not of those narrators in the present who use narratives of those events for present-day purposes. In its initial discursive position, the mitigation functions as a rhetorical frame which forecasts the forthcoming counterpoint of the post's own narrative telling.

There are three interconnected narrative threads in JAMES.T's short extract: an initial historical one, concerning the Black Douglas; a second historical one about how the Algerian War can be identified through actions and actors of 'the atrocities committed on all sides'; and a personal narrative encompassing the others. This third story is of the narrator reflecting on the actions of the Black Douglas with a question, before telling us that he has just finished reading *A Savage War of Peace*, causing him to reflect on why war and violence is valorised. Another post, by Duncan Kerr, makes a similar mitigating point, underlining the subjectivity of historical narratives: 'He [the Black Douglas] was a man of his period'. The rest of the post questions a straightforward reading of history, beginning 'what I find interesting is the extent to which the Black Douglas is being valorised for his exploits in Iberia'. This post is a reply to an earlier one made by Damien Kirk, also discussed above. Duncan Kerr's post outlines a narrative of the Black Douglas's crusading activities and a more general account of a 'sustained, centuries long, campaign to destroy what was, by most standards, the most refined, civilised and enlightened part of Western Europe: the Muslim kingdoms of Al-Andalus'. The main point is to question eulogising barbaric violence in the present: 'While its [sic] understandable, and no doubt good fun, to have rousing, national heroes full of martial virtue (and then some!)' and 'back then setting forth for distant lands to slaughter as many Muslims as one could was an act of uncontested virtue akin to mom 'n' apple pie'. These are, therefore, narratives of argumentation. Authors in this context are using multiple narrative types to modulate between discursive locations, such as the objective historical and the subjective personal, or to display their own position and critique those of others.

Conclusion

These digital interactions are readily available records of individuals' discursive bringing forth of Scotland. Giving deictic 'flagging' of the nation a wider definition and situating it within a narrative analysis allowed us to see that the discursive constitution of Scotland, at least by members of the public, is both diverse and argumentative in nature. Historical, personal and ideological narratives situate authors in complex discursive worlds, constructing the nation through the social, temporal and modal dimensions of narrative deixis. These different narratives of Scotland are used by authors as rhetorical tools for national argumentation, where even at the mass level individuals compete in the discursive constitution of the nation. As Rogers Smith (2003: 45) indicated, members of the public are not only advocating their view but also simultaneously constituting the nation by their discursive activity. Nationalistic narratives flag and situate the nation in complex ways, but personal and idiosyncratic inflections are also given to those narratives by their authors. One's nation is not merely banally 'here' and 'now'; it is discursively constitutive of stories about ourselves, stories which we may situate ourselves in, stand outside of or both. These are narratives of authentic national heroes from the distant past, narratives of a book about Scottish history read as a child or narratives about growing out of childlike readings of history and maturing into less atavistic, more rational and objective understandings. This interplay between the ideological, the personal and the historical demonstrates the complexities of identity, mediating between the individual and their personal connectedness to their wider social and political context. This observation is further underscored in the observations of Chapter 5's survey of mass opinion, in which it was difficult to 'pin down' any simple relationship between national identity and social class, political affiliation or constitutional policy preferences.

A diversity of opinion expressed through narratives was evident in the *Herald*'s online forum. However, the subject matter of those narratives tended to be non-civic in character. When constructing stories of the nation authors valorised neither the 'great Scottish educational tradition' nor the legal system, and did not refer to the Scottish Enlightenment. This could also be because the narratives available were written in response to the unveiling of a painting of a medieval knight. A newspaper article about Edinburgh University or David Hume might have elicited very different stories. However, stepping back and looking at the interactions as a whole, the debate represented a broad range of opinions. Thus, comments about 'English boot-lickers called London Labour' and a 'real Scottish hero' who chopped up the English and fed them to themselves competed with comments like 'I've long been troubled by the way we have celebrated some of the most awful things in our history'. Even though the icons of civil society do not form the basis of national narratives in this instance, there is a distinction which could be made between what we might also term atavistic and rationalist narratives. The latter are evident in those who draw attention to the subjectivity of the act of narration. Atavistic narratives were explicit in their commitment to non-civic cultural and historical conceptions of Scotland, while rationalist narratives are less explicit in terms of their commitment to the use of cultural icons as a basis for valorising the present.

7

The Scottish Political Elite View of National Identity

INTRODUCTION

Previous chapters have examined the rhetorical employment of national identity by the major political parties. Chapter 3 shows that significant changes have taken place, specifically changes in both emphasis and the terms employed to illustrate the nature and sense of identity and belonging in contemporary Scotland. We have highlighted examples that illustrate Scotland as a distinct nation of territorial location, and that illustrate the nation as a group of individuals resident in that territory. Such an identification has not been the particular reserve of one party or another; all major political parties within Scotland employ such rhetoric or imagery when they consider it prudent or necessary to do so, seeking to maximise the political opportunity at the elections in question. The most noticeable changes that have taken place have been those concerning the focus on a sense of nationhood and nation, of Scottishness and belonging; the idea of what the nation is has been transformed, as has the idea of who the members of that nation are.

Such a change has been most obvious within the Nationalist party, the SNP, although it is part of a trend evident to a lesser degree among all the major parties, be they unionist or Nationalist. In politics, the contemporary presentation of Scotland is that of a multicultural and multiethnic society, and Scottishness is predicated as a very inclusive sense of identity. The creation of a permeable border for the Scottish nation is apparent in any range of political documents and speeches. Coterminously, the strong sense of Scotland the place has become more pronounced, while the focus on Scotland as a distinct ethnic people has become much more limited. When politicians speak of the people of Scotland today, they mean the people *in* Scotland, not the people *of* Scotland – the modern parameters of the nation in terms of who belongs to that nation are extremely wide and quite encompassing.

However, manifestos are documents that represent the specific policies and attitudes of each party as a single unit. Although modern-day politics has seen an increasing personalisation of politics in the UK (Langer 2010), with political leaders placing an individual stamp on their respective party and bringing a new approach to areas of policy and direction, the party remains a mass unit that presents a series of policies which it hopes to adopt should it be victorious at the election for which the manifesto was prepared. Manifestos presented in Scotland are politically designed to gain support within and from the Scottish electorate in particular. While they put forward a political vision and a group voice for a party, they also, as we have seen, indicate party philosophy and ideology in other respects. This is both a positive and a negative in our investigation of the nature of national identity in Scotland. As a collective party political statement, manifestos do not represent the beliefs and attitudes of those who make up the parties. The collective party line may not tally entirely with a party member's or elected representative's personal beliefs.

This chapter therefore seeks an understanding of the sense of Scottish identity held by various individuals within the Scottish political elite ranks. Analysing individual responses on the issue of national identity, an understanding of their perception of the Scottish nation is sought. To achieve this conversational style interviews were undertaken with over sixty MSPs and Scots MPs, from all Scottish political parties with representation at these levels, in the period between 2003 and 2009. Each interviewee was given a list of possible questions, asking them to consider the nature of national identity in Scotland from their own personal perspective, as well as from a wider social and political perspective. As we sought to widen our findings beyond a simple reiteration of the established 'party line' we specifically chose to maximise anonymity and thus no responses are specifically identified, either politically or individually.

THE ELITE AND SCOTTISH NATIONAL IDENTITY

The political elite are individuals who provide the intellectual element of the governing group within a given society. They form the group to whom the masses look for pronouncements and statements about social and political issues of the day. Their importance within a national polity is also significant (Harris 2009), especially in Scotland, where elites had to 'invite the masses into history' (Nairn 1977: 340) and do so in a language that connected the elite and the mass idea of what the nation was. In contemporary Scotland everyday politics is a situation of contending elites who seek to construct a specific sense of national identity through their 'actions and discourse' in order to serve a clear 'political purpose' (Henderson and McEwen 2005). Established earlier, the prevailing scholarly view of Scottish national identity is modernist in approach, emphasising national identity as a constructed sense of identity (De Cillia et al. 1999), with a prominent elite influence and direction (Guibernau 2007; Henderson 2007).

While Guibernau and others recognise the masses as playing a role, the power of elites is always pre-eminent; however, this view overemphasises the capacity of elites to shape Scottish national identity. The ability of political elites to lead, influence and invoke a particular vision and version of the nation is acknowledged, but the idea of the nation as 'invented tradition' (Hobsbawm and Ranger 1983; Hobsbawm 1990) must be rejected and the power of elites reconciled with the power of the masses. Democracy is a set of procedures through which elites, charged with the responsibility for making important societal changes, can be called to account (Welsh 1979: 12) and it is through such a prism that contemporary Scotland must be scrutinised. Elites play a pivotal role within the national debate, but they do so within a 'pre-existing' framework as they seek to engage more widely (A. D. Smith 2001: 77). As the following discussion illustrates at various times, elites in Scotland are not operating on a blank historical, social or political canvas, but are attempting to harness an already significant level of national attachment among the Scottish populace. Nonetheless, the existence of the modernist position and the undeniable influence elites have indicates an ongoing requirement to consider elites, their individual attitudes and their understanding when examining Scottish national identity and it is to this that we now specifically turn.

In late 2007 the unionist parties within the Scottish Parliament created the Calman Commission. The primary purpose of the Commission was to investigate the authority and powers of the Scottish Parliament, but it was predicated upon the notion of Scottish distinctiveness, elucidating a vision of Scottishness resolutely allied to a vision of Scotland within the Union. In contrast and political opposition to Calman was the SNP-run Scottish Government's National Conversation, which also provided a political image of a future Scotland built around a particular concept of Scottishness distinct from the Union (Leith 2010). Such activities represent the ongoing, 'everyday' communications of leaders to the mass audiences, as contending political elites discursively and competitively enacting their version of national identity to garner support for their political objectives (Brass 1991; R. Smith 2003). They also illustrate the position upon which so many Scottish elites focus: Scotland's relationship within or outwith Britain.

ELITE SCOTTISHNESS AND BRITISHNESS

It was this ability of the Scottish elite to integrate themselves with the English elite at the UK level that dispossessed any nascent Scottish Nationalist movement of prospective leadership (Harvie 1994; Nairn 1977), as such leadership was instead provided to the British state. This is still the case today, although this positive for the Scottish elite may be a negative for the English in an age of devolution. A common complaint amongst several media (and political) personalities, most famously aired in 2005, was the existence of a Scottish 'Raj': a large number of elected Scots who held powerful political office at UK state level. As devolution had removed the day-to-day ability of English MPs to take direct action on policies impacting upon Scotland but had left the Scottish MPs in a position to influence decision-making for England (the West Lothian Question), the 'unfairness' of this position raised ire among the political elite of England. Whatever the reasoning for or actual validity of such a complaint, it illustrates the ease with which Scottish political elites have traditionally been able to engage in the wider British socio-political power structure and be part of the British political elite.

The issue of Scottishness, whether in contrast to or a part of Britishness, is at the heart of political discussion in Scotland and the UK today. Gordon Brown gave the issue focused attention on a number of occasions (Jeffery 2009). As a member of the Scottish political elite who held a position within the British political system he emphasised the connections between Scotland and the rest of the UK through a 'shared history' and set of institutions, arguing the continued need to enhance those connections. As an MP from Scotland he sought to engage with his Scottish constituents and the general Scottish public; as Prime Minister he did the same with the whole British electorate and public. This is an issue shared by all members of the Scottish/British political elite who operate within the now bifurcated Scottish political system. They must be both British and Scottish, as the issue of national identity in the UK is a political one (McCrone 2001). Gordon Brown's ability to rise to the apex of political authority in the UK was predicated on the possibility of him legitimately being British as well as Scottish. Such high political office may not be available to a Scottish politician in the future, as it has been argued that Britishness itself may well only be a political identity reliant upon specific political institutions (Willetts 2009) and as these institutions change, so do the opportunities available to the elite.

Scottish political elites seek to influence and direct national identity as a political force. The aspects of Scottishness (and Britishness) which elites draw upon for support are not purely constructed collective identities, but historical rooted forms that have determinate power with regard to the nature and activities of modern nationalist visions. In addition, political elites in Scotland operate within both a state and a national arena – where two identities are employed in the portrayal of competing political visions. While contending political elites may seek to influence the direction and aims of national feeling, they do so within a framework not fully of their own making. In addition, the fact that differing political elites in Scotland present inconsistent visions further limits the power of any one political elite group to present one unified vision.

Elite Perceptions of being Scottish and being British

Table 7.1 demonstrates that the majority of elites interviewed selected their identity as Scottish only, rather than Scottish and British, or British only. The results are roughly proportionate to those obtained in a variety of mass surveys carried out within the last decade (see Chapter 6) and the majority of elites interviewed identify more with their sense of Scottish identity than with their British identity.

Table 7.1 Self-selected elite identity

Elite identity	% response
Scottish	53
Scottish and British	31
British	7
N	64

Beyond such a crude statistical breakdown, there are additional results that point to the broad nature of national identity. One interviewee, after their initial statement, also gave their identity as Irish-Scots, rather than simply Scottish. In addition, Europe came up unprompted in seven answers, with respondents proclaiming European identity as part of their overall character – although several other interviewees added this identity when directly asked. One interviewee firmly stated that they were not European, and would never consider this as an aspect of their identity. Overall the European connection was very much a secondary aspect, often couched in similar language to that of being British: a state or legal identity rather than a national identity. This conceptualisation of identity as either state or national is not surprising given the presence the issue has had on the political scene and the discussions that have been ongoing in Scotland over the past few decades.

Several members of the elite were keen to stress a greater connection with a European sense of identity, rather than a British one: 'I'm much more comfortable being a European than I am being a Brit' (Interview 42). One answer, 'I'm a British citizen, my nationality is Scots. I'm also a citizen of Europe', (Interview 21) was very representative of the majority of comments in this area. This represents the increasing Europeanisation of identity that has occurred during recent times, as some political parties, such as the Liberal Democrats, have always advocated a strong Europe and others, such as the SNP, have shifted from a negative to a positive European viewpoint.

While seven individuals identified themselves as being British, only one interviewee rejected outright any sense of Scottishness, proclaiming, 'I am British, not Scottish, never have been' (Interview 35). Given the strength of national feeling in Scotland, this emphasis on Britishness was an unexpected statement and one not matched by any other subject. This respondent seemed to revel in providing such answers throughout but does signal a point that arose during several discussions: the problem of defining Scottishness. Some approached this problem from a legalistic perspective: 'When I see an entry in a journal I say, no, that's not right, you're a British national, because I am a picky lawyer' (Interview 54). Others were more politically oriented: 'I really don't see Scotland as a nation. Nations are sovereign, Scotland isn't' (Interview 41). Most envisaged the problem through such an official or legalistic lens: 'How do you define what a Scot is? I don't think you have hard and fast rules on it because it's not an official nationality' (Interview 19). Such statements are surprising, as these responses from the elite seem almost to deny the existence of Scotland as a nation; some individual elites appeared to deny the nation any formal existence beyond a territorial unit. When taken as part of their overall interviews, however, this was not the case. Specific language employed indicated the perception of Scotland as a nation and the Scottish people as a national group. Nonetheless, the majority of interviewees acknowledged that Scotland existed and being Scottish could be an aspect of being British, but both apart and distinct from that. Indeed, one stated, 'I always totally separate off the two' (Interview 7).

At the same time, a significant number rejected any sense of being British, many on a national and personal level: 'I would never see myself as British' (Interview 8); 'There is no such thing as Britain . . . [it] doesn't mean much as a nation' (Interview 12); 'I've never considered myself British and I don't quite know why' (Interview 11); and 'I don't accept British, as to me it has always had connotations I am not comfortable with' (Interview 47). These individual members of the elite rejected any sense of identity with the British 'nation' or state, let alone considering being Scottish as belonging to a national group within Britain. From their perspectives, Britishness has several aspects: it is not a nation at all; it is an alien identity to which they cannot relate; or it is an identity that contains aspects of belonging to which they do not wish to relate. Therefore, while elements of the Scottish political elite reject Britishness, they do so for a variety of reasons rather than because of one central or specific issue. The reason for rejection was this idea that Britain was not a nation but exists only as a state, a political unit. These respondents also rejected the idea of Britishness as a sense of group identity: 'I do recognise that we are part of the United Kingdom. There may still be a United Kingdom but there be no Britain' (Interview 6); 'There's no such thing as Britain other than the links between [England, Ireland, Scotland and Wales] . . . to me Britain doesn't mean much as a nation' (Interview 12); and 'I would see ourselves as part of a United Kingdom rather than a Great Britain' (Interview 42). Often linked to these statements was an acceptance of the fact that being British brought with it a prescribed sense of belonging, but it was little more than that: 'I recognise I am a subject of the British state, but I am not British' (Interview 49).

However, while Scottish identity is prominent among the Scottish elite, it is problematic for many individuals in terms of official definition and form. The state identity of British exists and is supported by formal structures – all respondents recognised that citizenship is conferred by the British state and one is thus a British citizen. Even those who would wish to reject this political state of affairs accepted that it existed in the current form. In the same way, the Maastricht Treaty created the formal category of citizen of the European Union – a fact acknowledged by many of the interviewees, strongly emphasised by a number, but certainly not welcomed by all. Nonetheless, possible confusion or lack of clarity did not hinder the majority from proclaiming themselves Scottish. The deficiency of a convenient formal or legal framework did not stand in the way of expression of a Scottish identity. Many of those proclaiming such an identity did so while rejecting any firm connection with Britain or a British identity. Many were at pains to separate Britishness and Scottishness – proclaiming the former to be 'very English dominated'.

Despite the inability to define a formal, let alone universal, definition, Scottishness is very much a given. When taking individual responses, differences between a non-Scottish 'them' and a Scottish 'us' were enunciated from the first. Initially, criteria for national belonging were formed from a position not so much of what individual identity was but rather of what it was not.

> I am fiercely Scottish in those aspects of my life that I allow myself to be . . . I feel a sense of identity . . . but if you ask me to say what . . . I am affected by the symbols of national identity but I am not sure I can identify it for you. I feel pride in Scottish institutions, I feel pride in Scottish traditions . . . I find it very difficult to define myself, and perhaps it is easier to define oneself by what one isn't and I am not English. (Interview 9)

This statement is representative of many responses, with individual elites defining themselves as Scottish by not being British (or occasionally English). Alternatively a significant minority of the elite did not feel the need to reject additional or supplementary identities when enunciating their national identity and saw little conflict in being both Scottish and British. However, the tendency, ultimately, was to stress their Scottishness:

> Well the first thing I would say is I'm from Scotland but I accept my passport says I'm British and I'm perfectly happy to be British. Proud to be Scottish but certainly not ashamed to be British and I would always say Scotland before the UK. Maybe that's not all that unusual . . . it would be rare I think for a Scot abroad to be asked 'where are you from' to say 'I'm from the United Kingdom' . . . they would say 'I am Scottish' or 'I'm from Scotland'. (Interview 10)

The majority of elite individuals saw themselves as being part of a distinct national group: the Scottish nation. While some saw this as conflicting with other possible identities (such as Britishness), others did not. What most had in common, whether accepting or rejecting other available identities, was that they placed their Scottishness first. But what is the Scottish nation?

ELITE PERCEPTIONS OF THE SCOTTISH NATION

How political elites verbalised their sense of identity was indicative of how they saw Scottish national identity as membership of the Scottish nation:

> My parents are Irish; I was born in England but have lived in Scotland for thirty years . . . My choice was to live in Scotland . . . my kids see

themselves as Scottish, I suppose what I am reflecting is that I don't particularly identify in the first instance as Scottish . . . I think it has to be, I think that Scotland, well the interchange, the idea of national boundaries, national identities is becoming increasingly blurred anyway . . . London is a melting point of identities. Although the inward and outward migrations are less in Scotland it is the same . . . I think the Scottish identity has to be flexible enough to accommodate these people and if it does not then it becomes retrospective and backward. (Interview 45)

This presents a viewpoint that equates fully with the modernist position in relation to the inclusive, civic view of national identity. They also present an argument that supports the idea that national belonging is less of an issue within the masses. The assertion is that being Scottish must incorporate a wide range of immigrants and second-generation individuals. The self-identification of the children of the interviewee as Scottish is telling on this point; while the parent does not choose a Scottish identity initially, the indication is that the interviewee argues for flexibility in Scottish identity but does not individually incorporate that identity themselves even while arguing for the right of others to do so.

Several statements present the fact that many members of the political elite were quite uncomfortable with placing boundaries on the national group, even at their own individual and personal level.

I don't wake up in the morning and feel the need to define [my national identity]. I don't have any feelings of a British national identity at all, but recognise a close affinity with the Welsh and Irish and don't view any of them as foreign. Scotland is my country, but that has evolved in time . . . but then Scotland has evolved quite dramatically in my lifetime. But I would be hard pushed to talk at great length about it, as I don't intellectualise it . . . I don't wear it on my sleeve. (Interview 44)

This individual was actually wearing jewellery with a specifically Scottish national symbol and therefore was wearing a symbolic identity on their sleeve that day. When pointed out, the incongruity of the situation in light of the above statement was met with amusement but such an incident openly represents an example of the banal aspects of national belonging identified by Billig (1995). At some point, this individual had chosen to own and wear such an identification of national belonging, yet had not fully incorporated such identification into their intellectual considerations on the subject of national identity. Nor, in the act of dressing, had they realised that they were reflecting an individual sense of Scottishness to the wider world. As an individual the interviewee strongly identified with Scotland and firmly rejected any sense of Britishness. Even while holding a strong personal identification of Scottishness (when other individual options were available) and actually, albeit subconsciously, engaging in a public display of that identification, this individual still exhibited a personal reluctance to verbally employ a distinct national label in the first instance.

Such findings involve several points worth bearing in mind in relation to our focus on national identity. First we must recognise the broad origins of the Scottish political elite. Many are born into Scottish families, others had Scottish partners and some initially moved to Scotland for employment purposes. In addition, several members of the Scottish political elite were born in Scotland, but to parents who were not. The comments from these individuals below are particularly worth examining. The second point is the continued rejection by many interviewees of any sense of Britishness. This is a point that arose time and again, reflecting a personal position more often than a purely political one. The third point is the unwillingness of many interviewees to provide any firm boundaries around the Scottish nation – although this was by no means unanimous. Many seemed keen to provide an argument that being Scottish offers a wide-ranging and very inclusive sense of belonging but it could not involve being British.

COMING TO SCOTLAND

Even a cursory consideration of biographical data reveals that a significant number of MSPs and Scottish constituency MPs who have held office since devolution occurred were not born within Scotland. This fact in itself provides evidence to support the idea that the Scottish electorate do not focus strongly on issues such as place of birth and national origin when it comes to issues of representation. A number of the Scottish politicians interviewed were born outside Scotland, and many were born to (one or two) Scottish parents. However, the majority of the political elite have a strong family connection with Scotland, even if they were not born in Scotland. Many openly recognised that this had some impact on their sense of identity and on their opinion of identity in a wider sense, although various interpretations occurred. As one interviewee stated, 'I don't really ever think of [national identity]. To be honest with you I don't bother about what nationality I am. I suppose if I was in a café in France I would say no, not English, Écosse' (Interview 48). This interviewee had one Scottish and one English parent, was born in England and made several telling state-ments regarding identity. Sport played a strong role in the framing of this person's identity. In football the individual supports England, cheers Scotland at rugby, but always wants to see England win at cricket. It was also emphasised by this person that a deep sense of national identity or 'pride' was important, but they did not see it going beyond the images of things such as tartan, haggis and such like – the 'shortbread tin' form of identity. The cultural aspects of Scotland were often quoted as a means of helping inculcate a sense of Scottishness, and T. C. Smout's often-cited interpretation of Scotland and being Scottish – that of a sense of place rather than tribe – was seen as the ideal.

Such cultural identification may provide reasons why individuals did not wish to categorise either themselves or the wider group as specifically Scottish or not. Many elites made similar statements, identifying themselves as Scottish but tending to stress Scotland as a place and thus present a territorial, rather than a group or tribal, sense of belonging. The implications are that Scotland is an inclusive society, where being Scottish does not require a birth-based connection. However, very few interviewees had no family or historical connection to Scotland, and those who did firmly emphasised theirs. This reflects an undercurrent of connection that could simply be available and thus used, or it may be that only elite members who have such a connection do not feel the need for it.

Other members of the elite, not born in Scotland, tended to stress the British aspect of their identity, although arguing that this was a generational as much as an individual aspect: 'I think that people of my generation born just after the war . . . it was stronger sense of British identity perhaps than there has been since' (Interview 7); 'We were a London family until my father brought us back . . . so while we always had a historical thing that we were Scottish, we were also a London family and so very British' (Interview 3). Such individuals also placed an emphasis on the multifaceted nature of identity, stressing the large number of identities they held. As one stated, national identity was a fairly complex issue: 'I would feel more comfortable with the Heinz 57 varieties description . . . I think you describe yourself as a different national identity depending on the context . . . national identity is far more complex than one word'. This individual argued that anyone can become Scottish by adopting the ethos and principles of the country they move to: 'you can take on the identity of your host country' (Interview 50). Although initially uncomfortable with any fervent sense of personal identity, this respondent indicated a strong personal connection with Scotland: 'we in Scotland . . . us Scots . . . we as a nation'. There was, then, a tendency for the interviewee to affirm membership of the Scottish nation, but when questioned directly on the subject of personal national identity they were reluctant to make that affirmation in forceful tones.

Many of the interviewees, while presenting themselves as British rather than Scottish, continued to argue for the right of people to consider themselves Scottish whatever their place of birth or origin. The majority of the elite were unwilling, even when including themselves in both the Scottish nation and a wider political grouping, to exclude any other individual from being Scots, should they so choose to be. This is in full agreement with the civic framing of national identity inherent in modernist interpretations of nationalism and national identity. We shall return to this specific issue of how elites bordered the nation later in this chapter.

SCOTTISH AS NOT BEING BRITISH OR ENGLISH

As noted above, throughout the interviews was the idea that being Scottish was particularly distinct from being British – even when the individuals recognised that they were British, or had individually identified themselves as Scottish and British, or British only: 'If somebody says they feel Scottish and British it doesn't take away from their sense of Scottish identity that they also feel part of something else' (Interview 5). Such emphasis was usually positive in tone: 'I think it enhances your nationality if you see yourself as [having supplementary identities]. I think it enhances rather than anything else' (Interview 28). Some comments on being Scottish and British rather than simply British stressed the manner of Scotland's entry into the Union:

> There is no other part of the Union that is similar to Scotland . . . there are a lot of similarities but I think there are fundamental differences . . . Scots were never conquered, or we were and regained our independence . . . most people who say they are Scottish would not boast about it as something narrow . . . some [Scottish] also feel British, so I don't think it's about being narrow. (Interview 1)

Not all interviewees were positive about the differences and many made it clear that they thought the differences were based on a dislike for the British state, or even the role the English played in what they saw as Scotland's 'subservience' within the United Kingdom. To one member of the political elite, there was a difference: 'I am not British . . . I am proud to be Scottish and have positive thoughts of being European . . . but Britain is a more negative identity' (Interview 49). This was not an isolated comment. Although it was a minority who made such statements, they represented a significant minority and were often unequivocal.

I feel not a single British fibre in my body . . . I am pro-European but it is not a strong part of my national identity . . . growing up it became clear to me that we are not equals in the United Kingdom, this was an English state and it bore no sense of identity for me. (Interview 27)

Englishness was identified as congruent with Britishness and it was this connection that often caused the rejection of British identity.

Others argued that a separation of Scottish identity from British identity was also part of the political system both old and new: 'perhaps from my time in Westminster, it was obvious that people identified which MPs came from Scotland and they could almost identify where we would unite in issues and when we would not, and that cut across the parties' (Interview 37). Many argued that the Scottish Parliament functions in a new, distinct manner: 'the way the Scottish Parliament operates, I think there are differences in style and attitude that are there [rather than Westminster] . . . partly because there is a heightened sense of different nationality' (Interview 27). These and similar statements were made on the premise that being Scottish was very different from being British and being English, not just in attitude but also in behaviour.

A majority of interviewees argued that the Scottish nation was very inclusive and that any who chose the label could be Scottish. There were no firm boundaries placed around the nation in terms of who could and who could not belong. At the same time, they contended that being Scottish was different. To be Scottish allowed them to operate in a different political fashion. If anyone can consider themselves Scottish, whatever their origins, how can being Scottish result in operating differently? It was on this issue of difference that the cultural, historical and even ethnic aspects of identity began to be employed by interviewees as evidence and justification.

In a similar fashion, many interviewees suggested that being Scottish was very different from being English, but most sought to do so on positive rather than negative grounds. This was the case in relation to the British/ Scottish division: 'I think you should be proud of whoever you are, Scottish, English, Welsh, French, wherever you are from' (Interview 33). Emphasis on dissimilarity between Scottish and British, or other groups within the UK, tended to be premised on the argument that Scots had different values, history or overall culture. Comments such as 'history plays a huge role . . . I think we are very conscious of our roots and history' (Interview 42) and 'We are a product of our past and our vision for the future. I think if you have a problem with the past that is a problem. If you are comfortable with where your society has come from there is no issue with that' (Interview 27) were regularly articulated. Whatever the basis for the belief in difference several elites argued that the distinction would always be made clear. As one summed it up, 'Everybody in Scotland, whether they consider themselves Unionists, supporters of independence, British, or anything else like, would never stay quiet if somebody said they were English' (Interview 18).

While statements such as those cited here exemplify the fact that elites recognise and emphasise the existence and distinctiveness of a Scottish national identity, our findings also consistently illustrated how elites would frame and conceive of that identity. The majority of elites stressed a very inclusive sense of identity, although this was by no means unanimous, as we shall now see as we consider how elected elites within Scotland frame the Scottish nation, and who can and cannot be considered Scottish and thus members of that nation.

A Nation without Borders

The emphasis within party manifestos on national identity has seen a shift over time towards a very inclusive sense of belonging and of all of the major parties none has made such an evident movement in this direction as the SNP (Leith 2008). From a distinctive idea of the Scottish nation that excluded certain categories, the party now presents a very inclusive sense of identity, where any individual who 'believes in Scotland' and resides within Scotland can be Scottish. Nor is the SNP alone in projecting this inclusive and civic-minded sense of identity. The Scottish Liberal Democrats, Scottish Labour and the Scottish Conservatives all provide for a Scotland that includes all the people within its borders as part of the nation, irrespective of land of birth or family origin.

Thus we would expect a similar pattern to be present within the elite considerations on what it is to be Scottish and who can be a member of the Scottish nation. Indeed, one individual commented, 'You will find it hard to find someone in politics who will argue the [ethnic/birth stance]' (Interview 45). This statement was made with the supporting argument that any other political position is not only 'off message' in terms of any major party and thus liable to get you into party trouble, but also unpalatable to most political and social commentators and liable to get you into media and public trouble. The majority of elites continually stressed the very inclusive nature of being Scottish: 'In the first place it [being Scottish] is a state of mind; secondly it is where you are. If you are born in Scotland, live in Scotland, have come to Scotland, are committed to Scotland; that makes you Scottish' (Interview 26). Here, one respondent gave a firm set of different foundations on which any individual could claim membership of the Scottish nation. The end result of this argument seems to be that it is simply politically unacceptable to conceptualise national belonging in any other form than a civic and inclusive one.

Similar comments also stressed the ability of any individual to choose to become Scottish: 'I think living in Scotland gives someone the opportunity to consider themselves Scottish if they wish. I think if you want to consider yourself Scottish, you should have that opportunity' (Interview 19). Another interviewee stated 'you can be . . . not of Scottish origin but have come to live in Scotland and you've taken on the Scottish so . . . it can be either nature or nurture, I suppose' (Interview 14) and another simply stated 'Scotland makes you Scottish' (Interview 16). These arguments sustain the civic, inclusive nature of identity, where nationality is an individual choice based solely upon a combination of location, personal preference and identification with the group. This modern, forward-looking vision of belonging rejects any idea of national identity based on birth, lineage or family history. One interviewee summed up the issue with the view that Scotland not only had a civic, inclusive sense of identity, but also would need it:

> It is going to be necessary that a lot more people who live in Scotland will be born outwith our borders . . . we will need that in the future. For me, if you're in Scotland and living here, you're contributing to our society either at the economic or social level, then as far as I am concerned, you're a Scot . . . It is about where we are and where we will be keeping in geographic terms rather than some great linear thing that takes us back into history so, you know, there are new Scots, Asian Scots . . . Eastern European Scots . . . they are Scots, if they want to take on that badge it is there for them. (Interview 6)

Many interviewees provided personal experiences to support this viewpoint. Several had individual family members who were not born in Scotland or close friends who had come to Scotland from other areas and argued for their right to be Scottish: 'I have a friend who is Dutch by birth, but has lived in Scotland since the 20s and thinks of herself as very much Scottish . . . I think most people accept you' (Interview 17); 'My grandmother was English and lived in Scotland definitely far longer than she ever lived in England, she felt Scottish, she was very proud of being Scottish . . . you can be Scottish without ever giving up or casting off your background' (Interview 5); and 'My wife was not born in Scotland and only one of my children was, but they think they are Scottish and so do I' (Interview 39). Thus, many elites had personal attachments to an inclusive position on identity, and the majority interviewed provided unquestionable and powerful language in support of inclusive criteria of national belonging.

Different Borders

Unlike the masses, who place more non-civic criteria on the nation, the interviewees are very inclusive in their vision of Scottishness. Where the masses, by a clear majority, see birth as an essential aspect of being Scottish this is not a view shared by these elected elites from Scotland. A notable divide between the mass opinion and the elite opinion thus emerges, especially with regard to country of origin. The majority of elite interviewees argued that non-Scottish-born minorities could be included in the nation: 'You can be Scottish without casting off where you come from' (Interview 5). Many seemed to support the idea that anyone, and specifically people born and raised in England, could be Scottish – if such individuals chose to become so. Comments such as 'If they wish I think that's a personal thing to them' (Interview 31) and 'we are as all-encompassing as we can be and welcome as many people to a Scottish identity who want to take it up' (Interview 19) represent examples of how most interviewed saw the point. In relation to how the masses would view non-Scots-born individuals, most comments were distinctly similar: 'Nobody in their right minds would class them [the English] as alien or in any way intruders or incomers. If they care about their community, I think that's the fundamental issue' (Interview 17); or 'all I can say is I think people are comfortable in their [identity] and I think they are pretty welcoming, God knows I've been in many a society where they're not' (Interview 21). While the masses, in the majority, rejected the idea that English individuals could be Scottish (see Chapter 5), members of the political elite of Scotland did not; a clear divergence between mass and elite opinion exists on this point. However, the elite were not unanimous in their ambivalence to non-civic criteria of national membership.

Despite statements on the part of the majority of respondents, and the assertion given above that no individual in politics would argue from the position of identity being an ethnic birthright, such statements were made by a number of subjects. Several of these statements reflected a belief in the importance of birth, history and other cultural characteristics: 'I am a Gaelic speaker within Scotland . . . the oldest ethnic sub-group within Scotland in a way, you can almost argue that Gaelic was the language that made Scotland. What really matters to Scotland, initially identifying Scotland is the linguistic root' (Interview 40). Here this interviewee focused on an issue that occurs in many Nationalist movements – that of language; however, there is no significant linguistic inflection to Scottish nationalism. Gaelic is very much a minority language within Scotland, and while support for Gaelic language programmes has broad political support in Scotland, it is not a core issue for any political party, including those for whom independence is a key issue, but is used rhetorically as a marker of Scottishness, as indicated in Chapter 4. Nonetheless, Gaelic continues to be a consistent issue within all the major party manifesto commitments, and several elite individuals interviewed cited it as an issue in their considerations of what it is to be Scottish.

History, culture and birth were raised once as important to national identity: 'What makes me Scottish is my place of birth, my beliefs, my heritage, my lineage, my genealogy, my upbringing, all of that' (Interview 1). Another respondent provided a statement of a birthright basis for national belonging, arguing that 'Nationalism is from birth. Past has passion and memory' (Interview 42). Such a comment conflicts with the statement made by the elite subject that none would argue an ethnic or birthright sense of belonging. However, the latter statement was qualified by the assertion that 'one must remember the rest of the world' (Interview 42). This individual, among others, argued for a more tribal and less territorial or individual interpretation of being Scottish. This subject of tribe did occur in many discussions, and the argument raised in the following interview was representative of a viewpoint shared by many interviewees:

> although the tribe is being diluted, and has been I think, particularly over the last 150 years, I still think people would see themselves as – they tend to say 'I am Scottish' rather than 'I am from Scotland' . . . So, yes, certainly the place is fairly easily defined and is more easily defined than the Scottishness itself . . . I think most Scots would appreciate the difference quite clearly . . . I don't think people who come to live in Scotland are Scottish . . . my view is that people should either be born in Scotland or born in another country while the parents are working abroad i.e. not emigrated but were working abroad. (Interview 10)

Therefore, some interviewees echoed the majority of mass opinion, although they represented a substantial minority in elite terms. The majority of elites interviewed felt that identity could be chosen by in-dividuals and was not proscribed to individuals born outside Scotland's territorial borders; this, however, was in opposition to the majority of mass opinion.

CONCLUSIONS

Through a series of interviews, the personal conceptions of national identity of the political elite within Scotland have been outlined. This includes their own views of individual national identity as well as how they envisage the Scottish nation and national belonging as a whole. The majority of interviewees saw themselves as Scottish rather than holding a dual identity. At the same time, a significant minority were very comfortable with holding a dual identity and see no issues of compatibility with being at the same time Scottish and British. Many of those individuals who classified themselves as British rather than both, or even Scottish rather than both, allowed that other people could easily hold a dual identity if they choose to.

The majority of Scottish politicians provided a very tenuous and porous sense of nationhood and national belonging. A majority questioned the idea that barriers beyond an individual's control limited attempts to identify oneself as Scottish, although this was by no means a unanimous viewpoint. While all the interviewees agreed unambiguously with a national identity connected to Scotland the place, the majority were vague in their commitment to a sense of a tribal national identity. Most avoided any such argument; instead, they suggested that Scotland had long been an 'immigrant' or 'mongrel' nation and that being Scottish was very personal and 'a state of mind'.

While many questioned the validity of the present constitutional arrangements, few argued that being Scottish was an exclusive category or should be considered as such. Several who argued, or accepted the validity of, an exclusive position on national membership dismissed such an interpretation as politically or socially unacceptable in light of the needs of a future Scotland. However, even those individuals who maintained an inclusive sense of Scottishness argued for a distinctive sense of Scottish identity within the United Kingdom. We are therefore provided with an apparent paradox in relation to being Scottish. To be Scottish is to be distinct within the other national groups of the United Kingdom and to have a strong sense of identity; however, the borders of that identity are permeable and any individual, from another group within the United Kingdom or beyond, may choose to become a member of the Scottish nation if they wish. The majority of elites interviewed argued just such a position. They focused on Scotland as an identifier, arguing for a distinctive group identity premised on choice at the individual level.

These findings provide a significant point in our investigation of Scottish national identity. Overall, the majority of these members of the elected political elite in Scotland see national identity as very much an individual choice. Belonging to the national group and having a sense of Scottish national identity is an issue of self-perception and self-choice. According to this view, any individual who moves to Scotland and chooses to identify with Scotland can and does become Scottish. This argument reflects that provided within contemporary political literature and is the modernist, inclusive, civic-based form of belonging. Obviously there are dissenters from this viewpoint, and examples of that dissent are given within this chapter. Nonetheless our interviewees, all elected in Scotland, would argue in the majority that Scottishness is not an ethnically based form of belonging, but a civic one, where membership of the community and a self-selected sense of belonging are the main requisites for being Scottish.

A divergence has emerged between how the masses and the elite envisage the nation. Unlike the elite interviewees, the majority of respondents to mass surveys place firmer, non-civic criteria on being Scottish. Being Scottish is not simply an individual choice and a person cannot proclaim themselves to be Scottish unless that individual possesses certain other non-civic attributes as well. There are limitations that history and culture, and the interpretation of such by the masses, place upon the elite interpretation of national identity and belonging. Scotland, having existed as a separate nation in its own right, and having a distinct and well-studied history, provides for a strong and vibrant culture which is also distinct from that of its immediate neighbours within the United Kingdom (Haesly 2005). The review of mass opinion challenges both the political party view and the general political elite view of the nature of belonging to the Scottish nation and of Scottishness. At the same time we can conclude that the mass opinion also challenges the civic, inclusive sense of identity as argued by the modernist school.

8

(Re)describing Scottish National Identity

There is a growing realisation that national identity is an everyday part of Scottish society and the Scottish political system. However, an open recognition of national identity, and the idea that national identity matters, is not just a product of legislative devolution. Rather, it is a continuation of Scottish-British politics during the latter part of the twentieth century and before. During the latter part of last century, two devolution referenda took place in Scotland less than two decades apart. While common in many democratic systems, referenda are recent and previously rare innovations in the UK. Both referenda provided a majority in favour of a Scottish legislature, predicated upon the idea that Scotland had distinct problems that could only be addressed by specifically Scottish approaches. This particular point of political reasoning indicates recognition of the prominence and strength of national identity as a political force with significant support. The increasingly nationalist rhetorical activity among the Scottish political elite, alongside the related (but dissimilar) activity of the wider public, culminated in delivery of a Scottish parliament and marked a new period in Scottish politics.

The first decade of legislative devolution has witnessed not only an expansion of academic interest in Scottish politics but also an increase in the study and everyday awareness of Scottish national identity. As devolution has continued to alter the political stage upon which the nations of the UK act, Scotland has begun to develop a presence on the international stage that is built around the idea of Scotland as a nation rather than simply a 'sub-national' component of the UK. The Scottish Parliament and the Scottish Executives/Government, have, over the past ten years, begun to more openly employ, through actions and discourse, the symbolic trappings of a nation, as Scotland operates as a distinct and particular political unit. This embracing of the nation and the associated imagery, downplayed by political parties and actors of the past, has been embraced by First Ministers and party leaders of all persuasions.

In our treatment of national identity and political discourse in Scotland over the past forty years, we have investigated the manner in which political parties have employed national identity within the political arena, as well as examining the wider issues of elite and mass conceptions of Scottish national identity and how this has been exhibited within both groups. We have done so in several related ways. First we gave considerable attention to manifestos of the Scottish political parties, both those issued for British General Elections since 1970 and those for Scottish Parliament elections. In undertaking quantitative measurements of these documents, we have been able to gauge the movement of the four major parties along both a nationalist–unionist spectrum and the 'traditional' left–right spectrum of UK politics, noting how the mainstream parties, including the SNP, have, during the time when nationalism became an open and intrinsic aspect of the Scottish political system, engaged with that core identity of the Scottish electorate. Our main goal in undertaking this particular analysis was to illuminate the depth to which the parties have employed the concept of national identity and policy issues closely connected to it as they seek to obtain support within the Scottish polity, ascertaining that differences can be delineated both inter- and intra-party over time. We also examined the support for such activity from below, examining the results from several major mass surveys of the past few years, allowing us to generate, alongside the political party measurements, a depiction of the nature of national identity held by those who form the Scottish nation itself.

Our analysis also included the discourse and imagery displayed within the more recent Scottish manifestos for devolved elections. Now operating within a particularly Scottish dimension, often for Scottish, rather than British elections, documents with a more Scottish voice are issued. Billig's thesis was taken up and the banal invocation of the nation personified illustrated. This discourse analysis demonstrated the habitual terms in which the nation is portrayed, unthinkingly, as a person and the fact that this includes the full gamut of human behaviours: thinking, emoting, being and acting. In these metaphorical representations of the nation there was no easy split between the civic and the non-civic, the inclusive and the exclusive, and the pluralistic and the particular. Furthermore, as the masses also discursively manifest their national identity in any number of public forums, and hold their own particular and individual characteristics of how the nation is manifest, we examined an online discussion, demonstrating the narrative creativity of individuals in the demonstration of their own identities. Here, again, we illustrated the dynamic and multiple ways in which the nation can be discursively situated, noting in this instance the interplay between historical, personal and ideological narratives which members of the public deploy as they simultaneously argue for and discursively constitute their nation. There was a plurality of opinion about what should or should not be used to symbolise national identity and the narratives told could best be categorised as predominantly non-civic, even atavistic; however, the 'rationalist' voices in the debates tended to question the historical assumptions of others, doubting the validity of using medieval knights as valorisations of 'true Scottish icons' in the present, rather than presenting equivalent national civic narratives.

When we compare and contrast the discursive and political activity of the political elite alongside that of the mass of the Scottish nation clear themes are revealed. All major political players employ, to a greater or lesser degree, nationalist language and other forms of nationalism as a part of their core political message as they seek to gain support from the Scottish electorate, but this cannot be described as purely civic and inclusive in nature. The employment of a nationalist premise or the use of nationalist language is not the sole province of the SNP; even those staunchly supportive of the Union use the tropes of nationalism in the political arena. In addition, our analysis has also allowed us to establish that a divide exists between the elite and mass conceptions and projections of the Scottish nation, a divide that has ramifications for our understanding of national identity in Scotland and for the political role of nationalism itself in the future of Scotland and the UK. The ideas of inclusion and exclusion and the relative firmness of boundaries that are, or are not, placed around the nation are consistent throughout the argumentation of the political elite; however, there is a divergence with the opinions and beliefs of the Scottish masses. The differences between the majority elite and the mass formation of who the Scottish nation embraces, and who is or is not Scottish, point to a central issue in Scotland today.

Beyond Civic National Identity

The methodological approaches we employed to examine national identity and nationalism in Scotland from a political, as opposed to a cultural or historical, perspective have been built around the examination of the civic/non-civic and inclusive/exclusive forms of nationalism. A valid criticism against the ethno-symbolist perspective has been that it leaves the political aspects of nationalism itself virtually unconsidered. Therefore, by employing our broad, multi-method and inter-disciplinary approach, focusing on the political arena and examining the political employment of national identity and the nature of Scottish political nationalism in the wider public mind, we have sought to address this deficit. The result is a challenge to a strict Scottish modernist interpretation of Scottish national identity, arguing for a differing consideration, one involving the non-civic and more exclusive aspects of being Scottish.

Nationalism has been a constant aspect of Scottish politics for much of the existence of the UK (Nairn 2000). Although it is only within the last few decades that the SNP has become a serious political challenger within Scottish politics and has provided a continuous presence in the Westminster Parliament, all political parties in Scotland employed nationalism as part of their political message before that period and have also done since. Since the late 1960s it has been the presence of the SNP that has kept the focus of contemporary politics on national identity, but the idea of Scotland as a distinct nation, with a different identity and the need for different political solutions has run throughout the history of the Union. Numerous groups, throughout the era of mass politics, have advocated a separate Scottish assembly/parliament, and while it may not have been an issue that cleaved politics in Scotland, national identity has never been absent.

Even when the 1979 referendum on the establishment of a Scottish legislative assembly was deemed to have 'failed', despite the majority voting in favour of such a body, the issue of national identity and political nationalism remained an ongoing part of political activity. While Westminster politics became more Unionist and centralised under Margaret Thatcher (Nair 2000; Pittock 2008) the non-Tory parties in Scotland managed to align centre-left politics with the national Scottish interest in the public mind (McCrone 2001). The 1980s, although a period of infighting and decline for the SNP, saw nationalism active in other areas of society and politics and this period witnessed growing support for constitutional reform, especially within Labour ranks. The practicalities of British politics and the voting system ensured that it remained the only party able to actually deliver any form of devolution to Scotland, as the Conservatives remained opposed, and the Lib Dems and the SNP remained marginal political forces within the UK parliamentary system. Alongside that continuing political activity in Scotland was a growing academic interest in Scottish identity and nationalism, as the issues of nationalism and national identity stepped firmly back into the arena of wider academic analysis, with events around the world, especially in Eastern and Central Europe, driving such interest.

However, the nature of that nationalism and national identity remains theoretically disputed. A general division exists, one which reflects a division within wider nationalist studies, between those who argue for the existence of non-civic and exclusive manifestations of national identity and nationalism and those who engage with and support a civic-based and inclusive framework. While such distinctions remain perhaps the most widely used when categorising nationalist movements or polities, the civic versus ethnic divide remains artificial and is consistently challenged as a blind alley for further research, firmly discarded by some as a less than useful methodological approach. Of course we have used these distinctions within our work because of their descriptive usefulness. The mistake lies in holding on to any notion that these categories are in any way exclusive. What the discourse based method above illustrated was the apparent habitual nature of much of the language of national identity. It is difficult to refer to nations without familiar, banal metaphors and tropes, unmindfully written or spoken in the language of politics. It is also not merely a case of flagging a presupposed national collective but also creatively placing it within narratives or casting it as a person with actions, beliefs and states of being. These stories and characterisations may, of course, be civic and inclusive in nature but they are just as often non-civic and exclusive, and, as Chapter 4 particularly illustrated, they may also be non-civic and inclusive, as well as civic and exclusive. The point is that while politicians (and academics) may explicitly affirm their commitment to civic and inclusive criteria of national identity, they do so within a discourse laden with atavistic tendencies, historical references and irrational collectivism. Even when the stories are about the heritage of the Scottish Enlightenment, proud educational traditions or respected legal institutions these civic narratives cannot escape an emotive presentation.

Unsurprisingly, given that they form the elected, representative portion of those parties, the majority of elites we questioned also emphasised and espoused the civic and inclusive aspects of being Scottish when asked about their personal sense of national identity and the wider sense of being Scottish. In simple terms, membership of the Scottish nation is predicated on the personal choice of the individuals involved. Should one choose to become Scottish, and if one is resident in Scotland, then membership of the nation is available, irrespective of birthplace, race or creed. Furthermore, being Scottish does not preclude one from holding additional, supplementary or dual identities. Individuals can identify themselves as Scottish and British, Irish-Scots, Italian-Scots, Pakistani-Scots, Indian-Scots and so forth. These findings are also reflected in the conclusions of most academic research undertaken into the area of Scottishness and nationalism in Scotland over the past few years (see Hussein and Miller 2006). Scottish nationalism is presented as a forward-looking, inclusive and civic-minded movement, based around the simple idea that all who seek to be Scottish may become so, and that residence in Scotland is the primary marker for a national identity that can accept dual identity as a regular aspect of belonging, although of late there is increased recognition among such research of the exclusive nature of Scottish identity held by many individuals. As discussed in Chapter 7, despite the majority opinion that emphasises inclusivity, a significant number of political elites recognised the non-civic aspects of Scottish national identity that, for many, form part of being Scottish. It is these non-civic and exclusive elements that the masses tend to highlight when asked about their view of being Scottish and belonging to the Scottish nation. These markers of ancestry and birthright remain important criteria for being seen as a member of the Scottish nation by a majority of individuals considering themselves to be members of that nation.

In this era of modern, liberal, democratic politics, any Nationalist movement operating in a Western polity must employ a form of social and political civic involvement, and Scotland (and the wider UK) is no different. There are few movements that operate on an exclusive ethnic foundation or that seek establishment of a pure ethnic nation-state, and these tend to operate at the democratic fringes. Scotland has never had a mainstream political party that has advocated such a sense of Scottishness, and there would be no positive response within the political or wider social system for such a stance. In recent times, while the SNP has sought to portray its political opponents, primarily the Conservatives but also Labour and to a lesser extent the Liberal Democrats, as London controlled, or even 'anti-Scottish', it has moved away from providing an ethnically exclusive sense of Scottishness, or any exclusive style policies for non-Scots-born individuals. Nonetheless, there also exists within contemporary Scotland the situation that a civic nationalism must still create a sense of national identity by which specific individuals can identify with the larger national group. An 'us' or in-group must have a 'them' or out-group in order to border the nation and present a separate sense of identity. A distinct sense of belonging, whether it be territorial, historical or cultural in basis, is required for the creation of a Scottish nation and a distinct sense of Scottish national identity. For the wider public, which is the foundation and substantive body of the Scottish nation, being Scottish means not being English, and that other groups are excluded, at least by majorities of that mass. It is this sense of difference that the masses in Scotland recognise as ultimately creating the Scottish nation, based on a common belonging, birthright and ancestry.

Obviously a spectrum of opinion does exist in Scotland and there is significant minority support for a much wider sense of Scottishness, one that includes more individuals than the majority would allow for, but the majority mass opinion diverges significantly from the majority elite opinion about the basic components of membership of the Scottish nation. However, such difference does not point to Scots being exclusive to the point of ethnic dislike or irrational restriction and rejection of other individuals that they deem to be 'not' Scottish. Any argument advocating that the majority of those holding a strong sense of Scottish national identity affirm a 'hot' nationalism which advocates separation on a purely ethnic basis is clearly not valid in light of the political support routinely registered at election time for all parties.

Just as this spectrum of opinion exists among the individuals of the Scottish nation, the civic versus non-civic nature of Scottish national identity must also be considered on a spectrum. Modernist interpretations of nationalism seek to place national identity in Scotland firmly at the civic end of that spectrum, portraying Scottish nationalism overall in the inclusive and civic-based form. Yet such a depiction disregards the existence of exclusive, non-civic components within the political and the wider public's discourse of nationalism in Scotland. Ultimately the Modernist interpretation of nationalism resists the presence of ancestral or birthright aspects of national identity, with the more strict interpretations decrying non-civic belonging as artificial with no historical roots of any consequence (Özkirimli 2003).

By focusing on the political components, as well as on the contemporary social expressions of national identity within Scotland, we have shown that a strong sense of national identity does exist within Scotland and can be found within all political parties, at both the elite level and the mass level of Scottish society. Such an argument no longer receives serious opposition. The idea of Scotland as being anything other than a nation, with a distinct national identity, must be a cornerstone of any study of Scotland; however, we argue that a view of Scottish national identity which over-relies on civic interpretations does so to the detriment of greater understanding of nationalism in Scotland and the political implications of that nationalism.

Political Understanding

Scotland now operates in several distinct ways as a separate political system in the UK. The most obvious of which, and one that has wide social and economic implications, is that Scotland does not have a two-party system. This point is important for any understanding of the politics of nationalism and national identity in Scotland. The divergence between the British and Scottish party system began during the 1960s when the Liberal Democrats began an electoral resurgence. This long-term political renaissance has culminated in the party emerging during the 1990s as the second largest in terms of Scottish MPs returned to Westminster and in it being a partner in two coalition governments in Scotland as well as in the Westminster coalition after the 2010 elections.

It was during the same period that the SNP grew in significance, adding a distinctly separatist brand of Scottish nationalism to the mix and greatly changing the nature of Scottish politics. Nationalism now became an overt characteristic of Scottish politics rather than the more marginal facet that it had been during previous decades. These decades witnessed the presence of significant group mobilisation, popular agitation and even marginal parliamentary attempts at legislative devolution, although all had come to naught in terms of tangible outcomes. As previously noted, there is a direct correlation between the emergence of the SNP, the (re)rise of the Liberal Democrats and the referenda on, and creation of, a legislature for Scotland.

The emergence of the SNP resulted in Scotland developing a distinct political space that allowed nationalism to flourish as an explicit force across politics in Scotland. All the major, and even the minor, parties of Scotland espouse some form of Scottish nationalism, even when this nationalism is situated within a staunchly Unionist framework. Labour and the Conservatives remain committed to political Union and the Liberal Democrats envisage Scotland as part of a federal UK; yet all employ nationalist rhetoric and imagery in their political messages and documents (see Chapters 3 and 4). They openly avow themselves as Scottish, firmly committed to a national vision for Scotland, in order that they do not leave themselves open to the charge that they are 'non' Scottish or 'London' controlled – a charge that is often present among the political rhetoric of the SNP and a problem the Tories have particularly struggled to come to terms with since the mid 1990s.

In terms of Scottish politics, we can draw three major conclusions from our examination of the past four decades. The first concerns the positional analysis of each party on the nationalism-unionism index, the second the ongoing discourse of nationalism within Scottish politics and the third the political nature of Scottishness itself. The position of the parties today on the nationalism-unionism index bears a resemblance to that in the early 1970s. Although the Conservatives are placed on the unionist aspect of the index, this is a very marginal placement, and their measured position is very similar to that of the other three parties in that they have all sought, in recent British elections, to downplay a sense of Scottish national identity, even while it remains an obvious aspect of the rhetoric. The Conservatives have certainly not reverted to their position of the late 1990s, when they displayed a steadfastly unionist position, one that resulted in the loss of all previously held Scottish Conservative Westminster seats. Likewise both

Labour and the Liberal Democrats provide limited policy considerations on openly nationalist topics, a position generally occupied over the past four decades, although national identity remains an undercurrent for each as it has done throughout. The one party that has reverted to an earlier pattern has been the SNP. From the 1970s onwards through to the last election, the SNP had become less blatantly nationalist in manifesto policy statements, with the party dedicating smaller amounts of space to purely separatist aims. This position was almost completely reversed in 2010 and a clear difference from the three unionist parties is now present. Nonetheless, a sense of nationalism is so widespread within Scottish politics that it is the preserve not just of one party but of all parties: whatever its specific policy objectives, each seeks to be openly Scottish and to employ a nationalist idiom reconciled to differing constitutional preferences.

Therefore, there exists within the Scottish political system a commitment to a strong sense of nation with a distinct feeling of national identity, which is not 'big N' nationalist per se but impacts heavily upon inter-party competition, within Scotland and the wider UK, in an complex matrix of wider economic, social and cultural policies and constitutional preferences. Although the constitutional policy preferences, as another reflection of nationalism, have changed over time and between parties, history, culture and birthright do play a role in the enactment of Scottish identity. In terms of the discourse of identity, when it comes to General Elections within Scotland each party presents itself as being Scottish. In 2010, the explicit emphasis of all parties is one of territory, with the primary aspect of belonging being residence. Scotland the place has become the focus and basis for most discussion on issues of national identity, with inclusion the political watchword. Politically speaking, being Scottish is now much more connected to a sense of place, a civic form of belonging, rather than any non-civic aspects such as a sense of history, tribe or birth. However, the real significance is in terms of when and how all the political parties have built this image. The framing of policies with the use of habitual metaphors of nationalism (the nation personified), and its metonymic extension to the national collective, flags the assumptive 'us' as neutrally 'here' and 'now'. This discourse of the national 'us' does not just occur as a neutral framing but one which routinely and unmindfully inculcates historical genealogies, cultural uniqueness and emotive sentimental belonging (see Chapter 4).

It is this lessening of the non-civic, the historical, cultural or birthright in the sense of Scottish national identity presented by the parties, that brings us to the third conclusion, returning us to the theme of inclusion and exclusion. Our analysis makes it evident that the manner in which Scottish major political parties espouse Scottish national identity today is very much civic. Scotland is presented as a distinct territory and the other aspects of Scottish identity are less emphasised. All political parties within Scotland attempt to project a much wider scope than simply history or culture within their messages in order to connect with the Scottish electorate. Yet the core documents of several of those parties have employed, to a greater or lesser degree over time, elements of cultural and historic values. In the Scottish Parliament manifestos we examined there was a commitment to areas of cultural policy, such as arts or language, that do not neatly fit within a strictly civic rubric; and, again, many policies whether civic or non-civic in content are often valorised in the emotive language of belonging.

ELITE AND MASS DIVERGENCE

The majority elite conception of the Scottish nation is one with a wide-ranging membership not premised on any non-civic or ancestral sense of belonging, allowing individuals to self-select membership, with residence as the primary (if not sole) component. This position was prevalent throughout our examination and discussion of elite commentary. Reflecting the position of each political party, the sense of Scotland the place, rather than Scotland the tribe, was the direction in which the majority directed their arguments and ideas and nowhere was this more evident than among the individual sense of identity of the interviewees themselves. Overall, being Scottish was seen as an individual choice. Any individual living in Scotland and identifying with the Scottish nation should be, according to the majority of elites, considered a member of that nation. Even when the individuals concerned shared their Scottish identity with other forms, such as British, this dual identity was not seen as invalidating their claim to being Scottish, although others took a contrary position on this point. In a similar vein, some members of the elite focused on ancestral, ethnic or historical aspects of belonging, admitting, yet challenging the majority view of a civic-based sense of identity. This civic sense of identity gleaned from interviews with elite subjects strongly reflected the perceptions of identity portrayed within the party manifestos. To be Scottish is to have a civic-based identity within the territory of Scotland.

The major political parties in Scotland present an inclusive sense of identity that is not predicated on any sense of birth, ethnicity or history. The elite members of those parties agree firmly, also generally accepting the idea that a dual identity, being Scottish and being British, existed and presented few, if any, problems for individuals. Being Scottish and being British is a standard theme throughout the major unionist party manifestos. It is a theme that remained present even when a greater sense of Scottishness and Scotland emerged during the late 1980s and 1990s. Furthermore, it is a theme that also became evident again after the devolution settlement came into force, and British politics returned to more 'traditional' policies as a focus. Labour, the governing party of the UK for the first ten years of legislative devolution, emphasised a strong link between being Scottish and being British. Even when continually emphasising its commitment to Scotland and providing an evident sense of Scottish national identity, Labour has ensured that a firm commitment to Britain and Britishness remained.

The perceptions of the masses in Scotland differ greatly from the sense of nation portrayed by each major political party, and the elites within them. The masses perceive the Scottish nation as having much firmer and more distinct boundaries in terms of membership. The non-civic aspects, dismissed by the elite and political entities as unimportant, are seen as central by the masses. The birthright component of Scottishness is very much a requirement that validates the claim to being Scottish. A majority of individuals who consider themselves part of the Scottish nation ground this belonging through direct or familial lineage and would deny membership to those who cannot. The limitations to inclusion are evident among the mass attitudes and divergent from the political elite. This conclusion directly challenges the civic interpretation of Scottish national identity and the modernist understanding of Scottish political nationalism and points to the limitations that the non-civic components place on national belonging.

CHALLENGES AND IMPLICATIONS

Political parties and their members are aware of the strength of national identity among the Scottish electorate. They are also aware that, within the masses, a sense of history, culture, ancestry and birthright combines to create a Scottishness that cuts across the political, ideological and social spectrum. This national identity at the mass level is an example of classic nationalism, which in significant part contains the grist of non-civic criteria. Whatever the basis for the connection, the masses in Scotland link to the idea of the Scottish nation through channels that the Modernist school would discount as significant. As a theoretical framework that envisages nationalism as a recent concept, modernism refutes an historical basis for nationalist attachment: 'national identity is a modern phenomenon of a fluid and dynamic nature, one by means of which a community sharing a particular set of characteristics is led to the subjective belief that its members are ancestrally related' (Guibernau 2004: 134). Modernist approaches do not accept that history also limits the ability to construct identity beyond specific boundaries. Each major political party in Scotland can choose to discount aspects of history, or even adapt them to its own political ends. The Conservatives, and also Labour, may emphasise 'British' historical events that connect Scotland to the wider UK, while the SNP focuses on events that emphasise a particularly Scottish projection, and there is no doubt that historical events can be selectively employed. However, as Anderson would have, nations may be imagined but that does not mean they are imaginary, and that goes for all the symbolic accoutrements accompanying them. At the risk of the denouncement of 'post-modernist relativism', an historical materialist thesis of the emergence of nations misses the point: regardless of whether past events happened or not, or whether past events fall within the desired timeframe, the discursive redeployment of the material of history is a symbolic reality of modern nations. The case of Scotland indicates that while individual political elites (or their respective political party) or academics may choose to downplay or disregard the non-civic, ancestral aspect of belonging, it is an important part of the individual connection to the nation in the mind of many of the individuals within that nation. However tenuous, claims can be and are made or implied for ancient historical roots; more modern stories of legal, educational or entrepreneurial traditions also rest on a narratological foundation reliant upon an acceptance of the value of tradition and heritage. As we have seen, political elites do use the stories and symbols of the nation, and if they did not then inscribing *flesh of my flesh, bone of my bone* on the wall of the Parliament building would not be a legitimate act of establishment patriotic allegory but instead a piece of radical Nationalist graffiti. The myths, stories and symbols available to adorn national monuments, denounce the unpatriotic or advocate policy are the product of historically and socially contingent processes, and as such have limits to their use.

Dismissal of perennialist claims to deep historical roots of nations is made on the basis of the modernist criteria for defining the nation. Nations are the novel products of global processes of 'modernisation' – 'the fate of modernity' in Nairn's (2000: 199) words, for example, industrial or print capitalism, the professionalisation of state apparatus or mass secular education, which are what Anthony D. Smith (2008: 2–3) referred to as 'categorical assumptions' underlying the periodisation thesis of modernism. Therefore, 'what' the nation is inextricably linked to questions of 'when' the nation. However, regardless of pedantic learned argument, in the discourse of national identity there is interplay between the civic and non-civic. All political parties in Scotland use a sense of national identity espousing civic-based values, not explicitly reliant on birth or any firm ethnic basis for membership of the Scottish nation. However, in the recent past, all, not just the SNP, employed a sense of history or emphasised Scotland as particularly different, and the latter is still claimed today. Modernism may be correct when it points to the employment of history, and culture, as providing a mould in which a specific form of national identity may be formed, but this claim ignores the limitations that that moulding may take, as the mass understanding of national identity places limits on the manipulation elites may employ.

The SNP faces a challenge to being able to lay claim to the label of being the national or Scottish party; all parties claim to be Scottish and to employ a sense of nation. The question is whether the SNP would actually benefit from a return to its previous manifesto style, employing a more emotional, exclusionary and ethnic-based rhetoric and creating specific exclusionary policies. Such a position may well appeal to a limited and minority core group of the Scottish electorate, but the connection between voting behaviour, party identification and national identity is so complex that such a move would not guarantee electoral results. Furthermore, such a move would put the party outside the mainstream of political discourse and leave it open to attack by the other major parties. Any possible gains are offset by several potential social and political pitfalls. Nor is the SNP likely to undertake such an activity, despite claims that since 2007, the party has modified its 'emphasis on civic nationalism' to one 'based around groups, some ethnic, others professional, directed by the state' (Gallagher 2009: 226).

The SNP also faces a dilemma with regard to national identity and nationalism, but it is not alone. The party cannot solely claim the nationalist mantle, and it provides a basis for national belonging on an identity shared with the other major parties. The only issue that sets it apart within this area is the separatist-focused stance on Scottish independence: an issue that is no longer predicated on any ethnic or cultural basis. The electorate within Scotland may not support such urges towards independence, as the masses do not appear to perceive of their national identity in this manner. The contemporary SNP message contracts Scotland as a territorial entity, and the inclusive nature of that message disbars ethnic or culturally based claims for independence. The SNP does not portray its vision of independence as a return to a 'golden age' of the Scots, but a 'golden tomorrow' of all the people in Scotland. However, this is the message also espoused by the SNP's political rivals, although in their vision, the golden tomorrow is of a proud, devolved Scotland within the UK. In addition, all of these golden tomorrows see Scotland as part of the EU. The connections that these claims provide to a sense of Scottishness held by many within the Scottish nation are limited. The image of an independent Scotland, as portrayed by the SNP, does not resonate with the image of Scotland as held by the masses. They perceive Scottish national identity through issues of birthright, ancestry and shared culture and history. There is limited support for the idea that being Scottish is predicated upon a purely territorial connection and this remains a minority view at the mass level.

Nationalism is a daily activity (Billig 1995; Kaldor 2004), whether that activity is conscious or subconscious. We have illustrated both elite and mass discursive 'flagging' of the nation in differing and intricate ways, including metaphor and narrative strategies. Yet they are not, as Kaldor argues, made on purely political grounds such as democracy. This may have been an element of the arguments in the late 1990s when the referenda on devolution brought national imagery, symbols, rhetoric and myths to the fore, but at the heart of the devolution argument lies the simplistic but informative statement 'Scottish solutions for Scottish problems'. The premise for Scottish devolution was very much identity based, as being Scottish was different. The ambiguity of national reference, be it through habitual metaphors or deictic referents such as 'our' or 'here', enables parties to connect with the differing mass, less inclusive, sense of Scottishness.

Kaldor's claim that 'the view that ordinary people need ethnic or cultural symbols' seems to us to be over-paternalistic (2004: 164) and may miss a important aspect of nationalism and national identity: it is, in part, a mass-driven phenomenon with attendant mass characteristics. This very point is one so often neglected, even among supporters of perennialist or ethno-symbolist style approaches. It is valid to claim that 'it is the elite who articulate political claims about the nation and put forward political demands. It is in the elite that concepts of the nation are shaped and modified' (Kearton 2005: 25); nevertheless, it is in the masses that the nation is given form and concrete substance. Various elites compete to provide their conceptualisations of the nation, seeking to shape or modify the nation to suit their political ends. But it is the masses that provide the nation itself. The mass conception of the nation, while being influenced by the elite political activity, also influences and directs the ability of the various elites to control the present. If control of the present is control of the past, as Nairn claimed (1977), then the masses control who has control of the past.

In mainstream Scottish politics, contemporary Scotland is an inclusive, multicultural nation, where membership is predicated on a civic basis. Even the SNP, the major party dedicated to the creation of a nation-state, with congruent territorial and political borders for Scotland the nation, provides a very inclusive image of Scottishness. When this conceptualisation of the nation is directly contrasted with how the masses conceive of their sense of Scottishness then divergence is apparent. Significant numbers of mass respondents to surveys have consistently produced a much less inclusive sense of Scottishness. The masses place more exclusive criteria on national belonging, creating a much firmer sense of who is, and who is not, Scottish. The nature of Scotland may be open to interpretation, and parties may seek to present specific views to support their visions, but again, the mass interpretation limits how far the parties and elected elites can manipulate or interpret. The ability of political elites to manipulate the sense of nation and national belonging is limited in the Scottish case. While the political elite present the nation in one form, the masses hold another.

The perception of Scottish nationalism through the modernist lens leaves unanswered questions. The masses within Scotland draw upon their non-civic sense of ancestry and birthright to create boundaries for, and belonging to, their nation. Political parties may provide a different view of membership of the nation, and may employ that view, but these are recent activities for several parties and have limits at both the mass and the elite levels. While the majority of elites present a modernist, civic-minded sense of nationalism and national identity, a minority made it plain that they held similar opinions to those of the masses. They too stressed the ethnic, historical and cultural basis of being Scottish. While a minority, they represent a challenge to the overarching view projected within the political system. Furthermore, Scottish political parties use non-civic conceptions of the Scottish nation, including history, cultural, tradition and language, when advocating policies connected to the wider cultural and social world. In fact, it is probably impossible not to ground policy within a discourse of belonging, history and culture given the pervasive remit of contemporary democracies. As Rogers Smith (2003) asserted, if politicians did not then their 'stories of people' would be much less compelling and civic-based stories alone are not enough to support a deep sense of national belonging.

No prescription for appropriately moderate forms of political memberships can be adequate if it does not explicitly address the need for ethically constitutive stories that indicate why those memberships embody identities that their members should embrace, even as they also support, enduring political moderation. Essential as they are, neither force alone, nor accounts stressing economic and political power benefits, will be enough to sustain viable and appropriate forms of political peoplehood over time . . . The necessity for these stories means that virtually all current prescriptions for embracing concepts of a purely 'civic nation,' or a purely 'constitutional patriotism,' some form of essentially 'liberal' or 'republican' or 'liberal republican' or 'neorepublican' or 'strong democratic' or 'social democratic' or 'cosmopolitan citizenship' as conventionally defined, seem insufficient. Although these perspectives provide indispensable elements that can contribute to a more salutary politics of people-making, they recurrently minimize or evade the need for ethically [that is, historical, cultural, ancestral and religious] constitutive stories. (R. Smith 2003: 132–3)

Parties that attempt to employ a sense of national belonging and identity that fails to connect to the mass perception, or parties that become identified as being 'anti' or 'non' Scottish have, unmistakably, suffered electorally. This may also be the fate of political parties that seek to present themselves as Scottish but employ a sense of Scottishness that is alien to the masses within Scotland. In conclusion, what we have been driving at is proper recognition of the non-civic aspects of Scottish national identity. The challenge, which has not been our focus here, is not the occlusion of what some considered the 'unsavoury' aspects of national identity but rather a better understanding of how the civic and the non-civic, and the inclusive and exclusive sides of identity interplay with each other and with wider social and political factors. National identity is not a fixed point nor some *a priori* essence; although, as we and others have shown, it may remain consistent and persistent in many respects, its relationship with other identities, such as Britishness, Europeanness and local identities, has changed, as has its influence on constitutional and policy issues, such as devolution and independence or the community charge or Conservative neo-liberalism in general.

Bibliography

Anderson, B. (1983), *Imagined Communities: Reflections on the Origin and Spread of Nationalism*, London: Verso.

Anderson, B. (2006), *Imagined Communities: Reflections on the Origin and Spread of Nationalism* (revised edn), London: Verso.

Aughey, A. (2010), 'National identity, allegiance and constitutional change in the United Kingdom', *Nations and Nationalism*, 16(2): 335–53.

Bakhtin, M. M. (1981), *The Dialogic Imagination*, Austin, TX: University of Texas Press.

Bara, J. and Budge, I. (2001), 'Party policy and ideology: still New Labour?', *Parliamentary Affairs*, 54(4): 590–606.

Bechhofer, F. and McCrone, D. (2009a), 'Being Scottish', in F. Bechhofer and D. McCrone (eds), *National Identity, Nationalism and Constitutional Change*, Basingstoke: Palgrave Macmillan, pp. 64–94.

Bechhofer, F. and McCrone, D. (2009b), 'Stating the obvious: ten truths about national identity', *Scottish Affairs*, 67: 7–22.

Bell, M. (1990), 'How primordial is narrative?', in C. Nash (ed.), *Narrative in Culture: the Uses of Storytelling in the Sciences, Philosophy, and Literature*, London: Routledge, pp. 172–98.

Bennie, L., Brand, J. and Mitchell, J. (1997), *How Scotland Votes: Scottish Parties and Elections*, Manchester: Manchester University Press.

Bhabha, H. K. (1990), 'DissemiNation: time, narrative, and the margins of the modern nation', in H. K. Bhabha (ed.), *Nation and Narration*, London: Routledge, pp. 291–322.

Billig, M. (1995), *Banal Nationalism*, London: Sage.

Billig, M. (1997), 'Beyond the production and consumption of nationalism: a reply to Kim and Wertsch', *Culture & Psychology*, 3: 485–91.

Bond, R. (2000), 'Squaring the circles: demonstrating and explaining the political "non-alignment" of Scottish national identity', *Scottish Affairs*, 32: 15–35.

Bond, R. (2009), 'Political attitudes and national identities in Scotland and England', in F. Bechhofer and D. McCrone (eds), *National Identity*,

Nationalism and Constitutional Change, Basingstoke: Palgrave Macmillan, pp. 95–121.

Bond, R. and Rosie, M. (2002), 'National identities in post devolution Scotland', *Scottish Affairs*, 40: 34–53.

Bond, R., Charsley, K. and Crundy, S. (2010), 'An audible minority: migration, settlement and identity among English graduates in Scotland', *Journal of Ethnic and Migration Studies*, 36(3): 483–99.

Bond, R. and Rosie, M. (2010), 'National identities and attitudes to constitutional change in post-devolution UK: a four territories comparison', *Regional and Federal Studies*, 20(1): 83–105.

Bourdieu, P. (1991), *Language and Symbolic Power*, Cambridge: Polity Press.

Bowie, K. (2008), 'Popular resistance, religion and the Union in 1707', in T. M. Devine (ed.), *Scotland and the Union 1707–2007*, Edinburgh: Edinburgh University Press.

Brack, D. (2000), 'Introduction', in I. Dale (ed.), *Liberal Party General Election Manifestos 1900–1997*, London: Routledge.

Brand, J. (1978), *The National Movement in Scotland*, London: Routledge and Kegan Paul.

Brass, P. R. (1991), *Ethnicity and Nationalism: Theory and Comparison*, Newbury Park: Sage.

Breuilly, J. (1996), 'Approaches to Nationalism', in G. Balakrishnan, *Mapping the Nation*, London: Verso.

Brown, A., McCrone, D. and Paterson, L. (1996), *Politics and Society in Scotland*, London: Macmillan.

Brown, D. (1999), *Contemporary Nationalism: Civic, Ethnocultural and Multicultural Politics*, London: Routledge.

Budge, I. and Urwin, D. W. (1966), *Scottish Political Behaviour: A Case Study in British Homogeneity*, London: Longmans, Green & Co.

Budge, I. and Farlie, D. J. (1983), *Explaining and Predicting Elections: Issue Efforts and Party Strategies in Twenty-three Democracies*, London and Winchester, MA: Allen and Unwin.

Budge, I., Robertson, D. and Hearl, D. (1987), *Ideology, Strategy and Party Change: Spatial Analyses of Post-War Election Programmes in Nineteen Democracies*, Cambridge: Cambridge University Press.

Budge, I., Klingemann, H.-D., Volkens, A. and Bara, J. (2001), *Mapping Policy Preferences: Estimates for Parties, Electors, and Governments, 1945–1998*, Oxford and New York: Oxford University Press.

Calhoun, C. (1997), *Nationalism*, Buckingham: Open University Press.

Charteris-Black, J. (2004), *Corpus Approaches to Critical Metaphor Analysis*, Basingstoke: Palgrave Macmillan.

Charteris-Black, J. (2005), *Politicians and Rhetoric: The Persuasive Power of Metaphor*, Basingstoke: Palgrave Macmillan.

Chilton, P. (2004), *Analysing Political Discourse: Theory and Practice*, London: Routledge.

Christopoulos, D. and Herbert, S. (1997), 'Scottish elite responses to devolution', *Contemporary Political Studies*, 2: 781–801.

Coakley, J. (2004), 'Mobilizing the past: nationalist images of history', *Nationalism and Ethnic Politics*, 10: 531–60.

Cohen, A. P. (1996), 'Personal Nationalism: a Scottish view of some rites, rights, and wrongs', *American Ethnologist*, 23(4): 802–15.

Connor, W. (2004), 'The timelessness of nations', *Nations and Nationalism*, 10: 35–47.

Cooke, M. (2000), *On The Pragmatics of Communication*, Cambridge: Polity Press.

Cowan, E. J. (2003), *For Freedom Alone: The Declaration of Arbroath*, East Linton: Tuckwell Press.

Craig, C. (1982), 'Myths against history: tartanry and kailyard in 19th-century Scottish literature', in C. McArthur (ed.), *Scotch Reels: Scotland in Cinema and Television*, London: British Film Institute.

Culler, J. (1981), *The Pursuit of Signs: Semiotics, Literature, Deconstruction*, London: Routledge and Kegan Paul.

Curtice, J. and Heath, A. (2009), 'England awakes? Trends in national identity in England', in F. Bechhofer and D. McCrone (eds), *National Identity, Nationalism and Constitutional Change*, Basingstoke: Palgrave Macmillan, pp. 41–63.

Cuthbert, J. and Cuthbert, M. (2009), 'SNP economic strategy: neo-liberalism with a heart', in G. Hassan (ed.), *The Modern SNP from Protest to Power*, Edinburgh: Edinburgh University Press.

De Cillia, R., Reisigl, M. and Wodak, R. (1999), 'The discursive construction of national identities', *Discourse and Society*, 20(2): 149–74.

Denver, D., Mitchell, J., Pattie, C. and Bochel, H. (2000), *Scotland Decides: The Devolution Issue and Scottish Referendum*, London: Frank Cass.

Devine, T. M. (1999), *The Scottish Nation 1700–2000*, London: Penguin Books.

Devine, T. M. (2008), *Scotland and the Union, 1707–2007*, Edinburgh: Edinburgh University Press.

Devine, T. and Logue, P. (2002), *Being Scottish: Personal Reflections on Scottish Identity Today*, Edinburgh: Polygon.

Dinas, E. and Gemenis, K. (2010), 'Measuring parties' ideological positions with manifesto data', *Party Politics*, 16(4): 427–50.

Donnelly, B. (2007), 'Painting of a forgotten warrior', *Herald* (23 October, online edn).

Downs, A. (1957), *An Economic Theory of Democracy*, New York: Harper and Row.

Dresser, M. (1989), 'Britannia', in R. Samuel (ed.), *Patriotism: The Making and Unmaking of British National Identity. Volume III: National Fictions*, London: Routledge.

Edwards, O. D. (1989), *A Claim of Right for Scotland*, Edinburgh: Polygon.

Fairclough, N. (1992), *Discourse and Social Change*, Cambridge: Polity Press.

Fairclough, N. (2001), *Language and Power* (2nd edn), Harlow: Longman.

Ferguson, W. (1998), *The Identity of the Scottish Nation: An Historic Quest*, Edinburgh: Edinburgh University Press.

Finlay, R. (2009), 'The early years: from the inter-war period to the mid-1960s', in G. Hassan (ed.), *The Modern SNP from Protest to Power*, Edinburgh: Edinburgh University Press.

Foucault, M. (1989), *The Archaeology of Knowledge*, London: Routledge.

Fowler, R. (1986), *Linguistic Criticism*, Oxford: Oxford University Press.

Gallagher, T. (2009), *The Illusion of Freedom: Scotland under Nationalism*, London: C. Hurst & Co.

Gamble, A. and Wright, T. (eds) (2009), *Britishness: Perspectives on the British Question*, Chichester: Wiley-Blackwell.

Gay, O. (2004), 'Thresholds in referendums', Standard Note SN/PC/2809, London: Parliament and Constitutions Centre.

Guibernau, M. (1999), *Nations without States*, Cambridge: Polity Press.

Guibernau, M. (2004), 'Anthony D. Smith on nations and national identity: a critical assessment', in M. Guibernau and J. Hutchinson, *History and National Destiny: Ethnosymbolism and its Critics*, Oxford: Blackwell.

Guibernau, M. (2007), *The Identity of Nations*, Cambridge: Polity Press.

Haesly, R. (2005), 'Identifying Scotland and Wales: types of Scottish and Welsh national identities', *Nations and Nationalism*, 11: 243–63.

Hague, E. (1994), 'Scotland as a place: an analysis of the SNP's 1992 party political broadcasts', *Scottish Geographical Magazine*, 110(3): 140–9.

Halliday, M. A. K. and Matthiessen, C. M. I. M. (2004), *An Introduction to Functional Grammar* (3rd edn), London: Arnold.

Hanham, H. J. (1969), *Scottish Nationalism*, London: Faber.

Harris, E. (2009), *Nationalism: Theories and Cases*, Edinburgh: Edinburgh University Press.

Harvie, C. (1977), *Scotland and Nationalism: Scottish Society and Politics, 1707–1977*, London: Allen and Unwin.

Harvie, C. (1994), *Scotland and Nationalism: Scottish Society and Politics 1707–1994*, London: Routledge.

Harvie, C. (1998), *No Gods and Precious Few Heroes: Twentieth-century Scotland*, Edinburgh: Edinburgh University Press.

Harvie, C. and Jones, P. (2000), *The Road to Home Rule: Images of Scotland's Cause*, Edinburgh: Polygon.

Henderson, A. (1999), 'Political constructions of national identity in Scotland and Quebec', *Scottish Affairs*, 29: 121–38.

Henderson, A. (2007), *Hierarchies of Belonging: National Identity and Political Culture in Scotland and Quebec*, Montreal and Kingston: McGill-Queen's University Press.

Henderson, A. and McEwen, N. (2005), 'Do shared values underpin national identity? Examining the role of values in national identity in Canada and the United Kingdom', *National Identities*, 7(2): 173–91.

Heywood, P. (2002), *Politics* (2nd edn), Basingstoke: Palgrave Macmillan.

Higgins, J. (2004a), 'The articulation of nation and politics in the Scottish press', *Journal of Language and Politics*, 3(3): 463–83.

Higgins, J. (2004b), 'Putting the nation in the news: the role of location formulation in a selection of Scottish newspapers', *Discourse and Society*, 15(5): 633–48.

Hobsbawm, E. (1990), *Nations and Nationalism since 1780*, Cambridge: Cambridge University Press.

Hobsbawm, E. and Ranger, T. (1983), *The Invention of Tradition*, Cambridge: Cambridge University Press.

Hussein, A. and Miller, W. (2006), 'Islamophobia and Anglophobia in post-devolution Scotland', in C. Bromley, J. Curtice, D. McCrone and A. Park (eds), *Has Devolution Delivered? The New Scotland Four Years On*, Edinburgh: Edinburgh University Press, pp. 159–86.

Hutchinson, J. (2008), 'Myth against myth: the nation as ethnic overlay', in M. Guibernau and J. Hutchinson, *History and National Destiny: Ethnosymbolism and its critics*, Oxford: Blackwell.

Ichijo, A. (2004), *Scottish Nationalism and the Idea of Europe: Concepts of Europe and the Nation*, London: Routledge.

Ichijo, A. and Spohn, W. (2005), *Entangled Identities: Nations and Europe*, Aldershot: Ashgate.

Irvine, M. (2004), 'Scotland, Labour and the trade union movement: partners in change or uneasy bedfellows?', in G. Hassan (ed.), *The Scottish Labour Party: History, Institutions and Ideas*, Edinburgh: Edinburgh University Press.

Jeffery, C. (2009), 'Devolution, Britishness and the future of the Union', in A. Gamble and T. Wright (eds), *Britishness: Perspectives on the British Question*, Chichester: Wiley-Blackwell.

Jones, R. and Desforges, L. (2003), 'Localities and reproduction of Welsh nationalism', *Political Geography*, 22: 271–92.

Kaldor, M. (2004), 'Nationalism and globalisation', *Nations and Nationalism*, 10(1/2): 161–77.

Kavanagh, D. (2000), *British Politics: Continuities and Change*, Oxford: Oxford University Press.

Kearton, A. (2005), 'Imagining the mongrel nation', *National Identities*, 7(1): 23–50.

Keating, M. (2001), *Nations Against the State: the New Politics of Nationalism in Quebec, Catalonia and Scotland* (2nd edn), Basingstoke: Palgrave Macmillan.

Keating, M. (2009), *The Independence of Scotland: Self-government and the Shifting Politics of Union*, Oxford: Oxford University Press.

Keating, M. and Bleiman, D. (1978), *Labour and Scottish Nationalism*, London: Macmillan.

Kellas, J. G. (1973), *The Scottish Political System*, Cambridge: Cambridge University Press.

Kellas, J. G. (1984), *The Scottish Political System* (3rd edn), Cambridge: Cambridge University Press.

Kiely, R., Bechhofer, F., Stewart, R. and McCrone, D. (2001), 'The markers and rules of Scottish national identity', *Sociological Review*, 49(1): 33–55.

Klingemann, H.-D., Volkens, A., Bara, J. and Budge, I. (2006), *Mapping Policy Preferences II: Estimates for Parties, Electors, and Governments in Eastern Europe, European Union and OECD 1990–2003*, Oxford: Oxford University Press.

Kövecses, Z. (2002), *Metaphor: A Practical Introduction*, Oxford: Oxford University Press.

Lakoff, G. (1987), *Women, Fire and Dangerous Things: What Categories Reveal About the Mind*, Chicago: Chicago University Press.

Lakoff, G. (2002), *Moral Politics: How Liberals and Conservatives Think*, Chicago: Chicago University Press.

Lakoff, G. and Johnson, M. (1980), *Metaphors We Live By*, Chicago: Chicago University Press.

Lamarque, P. (1990), 'Narrative and invention: the limits of fictionality', in C. Nash (ed.), *Narrative in Culture: The Uses of Storytelling in the Sciences, Philosophy, and Literature*, London: Routledge, pp. 131–53.

Langer, A. (2010), 'The politicization of private persona: exceptional leaders or the new rule? The case of the United Kingdom and the Blair effect', *International Journal of Press/Politics*, 15(1): 60–76.

Laver, M. J. and Budge, I. (1992), *Party Policy and Government Coalitions*, Basingstoke: Palgrave Macmillan.

Law, A. (2001), 'Near and far: banal national identity and the press in Scotland', *Media, Culture and Society*, 23: 299–317.

Leith, M. (2008), 'Scottish National Party representations of Scottishness and Scotland', *Politics*, 28(2): 83–92.

Leith, M. (2010), 'Governance and identity in a devolved Scotland', *Parliamentary Affairs*, 63(2): 286–301.

Leith, M. and Steven, M. (2010), 'Party over policy? Scottish Nationalism and the politics of independence', *The Political Quarterly*, 81(2): 263–9.

Lynch, P. (2002), *SNP: The History Of The Scottish National Party*, Cardiff: Welsh Academic Press.

MacInnes, J., Rosie, M., Petersoo, P. and Condor, S. (2004), 'Nation speaking unto nation? Newspapers and national identity in the devolved UK', *The Sociological Review*, 52(4): 437–58.

MacInnes, J., Rosie, M., Petersoo, P., Condor, S. and Kennedy, J. (2007), 'Where is the British national press?', *The British Journal of Sociology*, 58(2): 185–206.

Marquand, D. (1997), *The New Reckoning: Capitalism, States and Citizens*, Cambridge: Polity Press in association with the *New Statesman*.

McArthur, C. (1982), 'Scotland and cinema: the iniquity of the fathers', in C. McArthur (ed.), *Scotch Reels: Scotland in Cinema and Television*, London: British Film Institute.

McCrone, D. (2001), *Understanding Scotland: The Sociology of a Nation* (2nd edn), London: Routledge.

McCrone, D. and Bechhofer, F. (2010), 'Claiming national identity', *Ethnic and Racial Studies*, 33(6): 921–48.

McCrone, D., Stewart, R., Kiely, R. and Bechhofer, F. (1998), 'Who are we? Problematising national identity', *The Sociological Review*, 46(4): 629–52.

McEwen, N. (2002), 'State welfare nationalism: the territorial impact of welfare state development in Scotland', *Regional and Federal Studies*, 12(1): 66–90.

McGarvey, N. and Cairney, P. (2008), *Scottish Politics: an Introduction*, Basingstoke: Palgrave Macmillan.

McLean, I. (2006), 'The dimensionality of party ideologies', in J. Bara and A. Weale (eds), *Democratic Politics and Party Competition*, London: Routledge.

McLuhan, M. (1962), *The Gutenberg Galaxy: The Making of Typographic Man*, Toronto: University of Toronto Press.

Miller, W. L. (1981), *The End of British Politics?: Scots and English Political Behaviour in the Seventies*, Oxford: Clarendon Press.

Mitchell, J. (1996), *Strategies for Self-government: The Campaigns for a Scottish Parliament*, Edinburgh: Polygon.

Mitchell, J. (2003), *Governing Scotland: The Invention of Administrative Devolution*, Basingstoke: Palgrave Macmillan.

Mitchell, J. (2009), *Devolution in the UK*, Manchester: Manchester University Press.

Morton, G. (1999), *Unionist-Nationalism: Governing Urban Scotland*, East Linton: Tuckwell Press.

Nairn, T. (1977), *The Break-Up of Britain: Crisis and Neo-Nationalism*, London: NLB.

Nairn, T. (1981), *The Break-Up of Britain: Crisis and Neo-Nationalism* (2nd edn), London: Verso.

Nairn, T. (1997), *Faces of Nationalism: Janus Revisited*, London: Verso.

Nairn, T. (2000), *After Britain: New Labour and the Return of Scotland*, London: Granta.

Ong, W. J. (1982), *Orality and Literacy: The Technologizing of the World*, London: Routledge.

Özkirimli, U. (2003), 'The nation as an artichoke? A critique of ethno-symbolist interpretations of nationalism', *Nations and Nationalism* 9: 339–55.

Özkirimli, U. (2010), *Theories of Nationalism: A Critical Introduction* (2nd edn), Basingstoke: Palgrave Macmillan.

Paterson, L. (1994), *The Autonomy of Modern Scotland*, Edinburgh: Edinburgh University Press.

Paterson, L. (1999), 'Why should we respect civic Scotland?', in G. Hassan and C. Warhurst (eds), *A Moderniser's Guide to Scotland: A Different Future*, Glasgow: Big Issue in Scotland and Centre for Scottish Public Policy.

Paterson, L., Bechhofer, F. and McCrone, D. (2004), *Living in Scotland: Social and Economic Change since 1980*, Edinburgh: Edinburgh University Press.

Pelizzo, R. (2003), 'Party positions or party direction? An analysis of party manifesto data', *West European Politics*, 26: 67–89.

Petersoo, P. (2007), 'What does "we" mean?: National deixis in the media', *Journal of Language and Politics* 6(3): 419–36.

Pittock, M. (2008), *The Road To Independence? Scotland Since the Sixties*, London: Reaktion.

Renan, E. (1990) [1882], 'What is a nation?', in H. K. Bhabha (ed.), *Nation and Narration*, London: Routledge.

Rokkan, S. and Urwin, D. W. (1983), *Economy Territory Identity: Politics of West European Peripheries*, London: Sage.

Rosenbaum, M. (1997), *From Soapbox to Soundbite: Party Political Campaigning in Britian since 1945*, Basingstoke: Macmillan.

Rosie, M., MacInnes, J., Petersoo, P., Condon, S. and Kennedy, J. (2004), 'Nation speaking unto nation? Newspapers and national identity in the devolved UK', *Sociological Review*, 52(4): 437–58.

Rosie, M., Petersoo, P., MacInnes, J., Condor, S. and Kennedy, J. (2006), 'Mediating which nation? Citizenship and national identity in the British press', *Social Semiotics*, 16(2): 327–44.

Scotland Against Racism (2009), http://www.scotlandagainstracism.com/onescotland/22.1.6.html, accessed 4 March 2010.

Scottish Conservative Party (1970), *The Scottish Conservative Party Manifesto, Tomorrow's Scotland*.

Scottish Conservative Party (1974), *The Conservative Party Manifesto for Scotland*.

Scottish Conservative Party (1979), *The Conservative Manifesto for Scotland*.

Scottish Conservative Party (1983), *The Conservative Manifesto for Scotland*.

Scottish Conservative Party (1992), *The Scottish Conservative Party Manifesto, The Best Future for Scotland*.

Scottish Conservative Party (1997), *The Scottish Conservative Party Manifesto, Fighting for Scotland*.

Scottish Conservative Party (1999), *Scottish Conservative Party Manifesto: Scotland First*.

Scottish Conservative Party (2001), *The Conservative Party Manifesto, Time for Common Sense for Scotland*.

Scottish Conservative Party (2003), *Scottish Conservative Party Manifesto: Time To Do Something About It*.

Scottish Conservative Party (2005), *The Conservative Party Manifesto, Are you Thinking What We're Thinking? It's Time for Action*.

Scottish Conservative Party (2007), *Scottish Conservative Party Manifesto: Your Voice in Parliament*.

Scottish Conservative Party (2010), *Scottish Conservative Party Manifesto: Invitation to Join the Government of Britain*.

Scottish Government (2007), First Minister Alex Salmond, Northern Ireland Assembly, Stormont, Belfast, 18 June 2007, www.scotland.gov.uk/News/This-Week/Speeches/fmstormont, accessed 23 June 2008.

Scottish Labour Party (1979), *The Labour Party Manifesto, The Better Way for Scotland*.

Scottish Labour Party (1983), *The Labour Party Manifesto, The New Hope for Scotland*.

Scottish Labour Party (1987), *The Labour Party Manifesto, Scotland Will Win With Labour*.

Scottish Labour Party (1992), *The Labour Party Manifesto, It's Time to get Scotland Moving Again*.

Scottish Labour Party (1997), *The Labour Party Manifesto, New Labour Because Scotland Deserves Better*.

Scottish Labour Party (1999), *Scottish Labour Party Manifesto, Building Scotland's Future*.

Scottish Labour Party (2001), *The Labour Party Manifesto, Ambitions for Scotland*.

Scottish Labour Party (2003), *Scottish Labour Party Manifesto: On Your Side*.

Scottish Labour Party (2005), *The Labour Party Manifesto, Scotland Forward, Not Back*.

Scottish Labour Party (2007), *Scottish Labour Party Manifesto: Building Scotland*.

Scottish Labour Party (2010), *Scottish Labour Party Manifesto, A Future Fair for All*.

Scottish Liberal Democratic Party (1999), *Scottish Liberal Democratic Party Manifesto, Raising the Standards for our Schools, our Hospitals, our Jobs for Scotland's Future*.

Scottish Liberal Democratic Party (2003), *Scottish Liberal Democrats Party Manifesto, Make the Difference*.

Scottish Liberal Democrats (1997), *The Scottish Liberal Democrat Manifesto, Make The Difference*.

Scottish Liberal Democrats (2001), *The Scottish Liberal Democrat Manifesto, For a Liberal and Democratic Scotland*.

Scottish Liberal Democrats (2005), *The Scottish Liberal Democrat Manifesto, The Real Alternative*.

Scottish Liberal Democrats (2007), *Scottish Liberal Democratic Party Manifesto, We Think Scotland Has a Bright Future*.

Scottish Liberal Democrats (2010), *The Scottish Liberal Democrat Manifesto, Change that Works For You*.

Scottish Liberal Party (1979), *The Scottish Liberal Manifesto*.

Scottish National Party (1970), *SNP Manifesto, The New Scotland*.

Scottish National Party (1974), *Scotland's Future*.

Scottish National Party (1983), *SNP Manifesto, Choose Scotland – The Challenge of Independence*.

Scottish National Party (1987), *The SNP Manifesto, Play the Scottish Card*.

Scottish National Party (1992), *The SNP Manifesto, Independence in Europe – Make It Happen Now*.

Scottish National Party (1997), *The SNP Manifesto, YES WE CAN Win the Best for Scotland*.

Scottish National Party (1999), *SNP Manifesto, Scotland's Party*.

Scottish National Party (2001), *SNP Manifesto, We Stand for Scotland*.

Scottish National Party (2003), *SNP Manifesto, The Complete Case for a Better Scotland*.

Scottish National Party (2005), *SNP Manifesto, If Scotland Matters to you Make it Matter in May*.

Scottish National Party (2007), *SNP Manifesto, It's Time*.

Scottish National Party (2010), *SNP Manifesto, Elect a Local Champion*.

Scottish Social and Liberal Democrats (1983), *The Social and Liberal Democrats Manifesto, Working Together for Scotland*.

Scottish Social and Liberal Democrats (1987), *The Social and Liberal Democrats Manifesto, The Time Has Come for Scotland*.

Shelestiuk, H. V. (2006), 'Approaches to metaphor: structure, classifications, cognate phenomena', *Semiotica*, 161(1/4): 333–43.

Shotter, J. (1993), *Cultural Politics of Everyday Life: Social Constructionism, Rhetoric and Knowing of the Third Kind*, Buckingham: Open University Press.

Simpson, P. (1993), *Language, Ideology and Point of View*, London: Routledge.

Smith, A. D. (1986), *The Ethnic Origins of Nations*, Oxford: Basil Blackwell.

Smith, A. D. (1991), *National Identity*, London: Penguin.

Smith, A. D. (1998), *Nationalism and Modernism*, London: Routledge.

Smith, A. D. (2001), *Nationalism, Theory, Ideology, History*, Cambridge: Polity Press.

Smith, A. D. (2003), 'The poverty of anti-nationalist modernism', *Nations and Nationalism*, 9: 357–70.

Smith, A. D. (2008), *The Cultural Foundations of Nations: Hierarchy, Covenant and Republic*, Oxford: Blackwell.

Smith, R. (2003), *Stories of Peoplehood: The Politics and Morals of Political Membership*, Cambridge: Cambridge University Press.

Smout, T. C. (1969), *A History of the Scottish People, 1560–1830*, London: Collins.

Surel, J. (1989), 'John Bull', in R. Samuel (ed.), *Patriotism: The Making and Unmaking of British National Identity. Volume III: National Fictions*, London: Routledge.

Swales, J. M. (1990), *Genre Analysis: English in Academic and Research Settings*, Cambridge: Cambridge University Press.

Taylor, J. R. (1995), *Linguistic Categorization: Prototypes in Linguistic Theory* (2nd edn), Oxford: Oxford University Press.

Watson, M. (2003), *Being English in Scotland*, Edinburgh: Edinburgh University Press.

Webb, K. (1977), *The Growth of Nationalism in Scotland*, Harmondsworth: Penguin Books.

Welsh, W. A. (1979), *Leaders and Elites*, London: Holt, Rhinehart and Winston.

Willetts, D. (2009), 'England and Britain, Europe and the Anglosphere', *Political Quarterly*, 78(s1): 54–61.

Wodak, R., De Cillia, R., Reisigl, M. and Liebhart K. (1999), *The Discursive Construction of National Identity*, Edinburgh: Edinburgh University Press.

Appendix

Methodological Approach to Manifesto Coding
(Chapter 3 Methodology)

The method of quantitative content analysis employed by the CMP and utilised in modified form within this work allows for an analysis of the policies, issues, ideas and positions taken by Scottish political parties within their electoral platforms as contained within the manifestos presented for British General Elections. The original CMP framework contains fifty-six distinct categories, assembled into seven major policy domains. Our modified coding system added seven additional categories, providing sixty-three overall, within the original seven major policy domains. These domains and categories are listed below, with the additional categories included.

The coding procedures provided by the CMP state that the 'coding unit in a given programme is the "quasi-sentence", defined as an argument – that is the verbal expression of one political idea or issue . . . a quasi-sentence is a set of words containing one, and only one, political idea' (Klingemann et al. 2006: 165–6). Each manifesto is thus coded by breaking down the text into quasi-sentences, each expressing one distinct political idea/statement. These quasi-sentences are then allocated to an individual category within the coding framework. Visual aspects of manifestos, such as figures, tables, headings and other such content are not coded. Likewise, forewords or statements by party leaders are not coded, as they are considered the statements not of parties but of individuals.

The total number of quasi-sentences is the complete unit of analysis, and it is this total against which individual measurements of the various categories and domains can be undertaken and comparative assessments made. A fuller description of the method and instructions for its application and use can be found in Appendix II of Klingemann et al. (2006).

Domains

Domain 1: External Relations
Domain 2: Freedom and Democracy
Domain 3: Political System
Domain 4: Economy
Domain 5: Welfare and Quality of Life
Domain 6: Fabric of Society
Domain 7: Social Groups

Category (Code) No.	Category
101	Foreign special relationship positive
102	Foreign special relationship negative
103	Decolonisation
104	Military positive
105	Military negative
106	Peace
107	Internationalism positive
108	EU positive
109	Internationalism negative
110	EU negative
201	Freedom and domestic human rights
202	Democracy
203	Constitutionalism positive
204	Constitutionalism negative
205	Union positive
206	Union negative
207	Devolution positive
208	Devolution negative
301	Decentralisation
302	Centralisation
303	Government efficiency
304	Government corruption
305	Government effectiveness and authority
401	Free enterprise
402	Incentives
403	Regulation of capitalism
404	Economic planning
405	Corporatism
406	Protectionism positive
407	Protectionism negative

408	Economic goals
409	Keynesian demand management
410	Productivity
411	Technology and infrastructure
412	Controlled economy
413	Nationalisation
414	Economic orthodoxy
415	Marxist analysis
416	Anti-growth economy
501	Environmental protection
502	Arts, sports, leisure, media
503	Social justice
504	Social service expansion
505	Social service limitation
506	Education expansion
507	Education limitation
601	National way of life British
602	National way of life Scottish
603	Traditional morality positive
604	Traditional morality negative
605	Law and order
606	National effort and social harmony
607	Multiculturalism positive
608	Multiculturalism negative
609	Historical/mythical reference
610	Scotland's future reference
611	Scotland's past reference
701	Labour groups positive
702	Labour groups negative
703	Agriculture
704	Middle-class and professional groups
705	Minority groups
706	Non-economic demographic groups

Index

Note: f signifies Figure, t signifies Table

'A Claim of Right for Scotland' (1988), 33, 34
Anderson, B., 1, 10, 15, 67, 76, 100, 104, 150
Aughey, A., 23

Bakhtin, M. M., 79
banal nationalism, 13, 62, 67, 100–2, 128, 140
Bara, J., 48, 49–50
Barrie, J. M., 2
Bechhofer, F., 5, 87, 88, 94, 99, 103
Bell, M., 11
belonging, sense of national, 4, 80, 82, 87–98, 144, 148
Bennie, L., 18, 47
Bhabha, H. K., 11
Billig, M., 7, 10, 67, 71, 80, 100–2, 128, 140, 152
Black Douglas article (*Herald*, 2007), online discussion threads, 106–18
Bleiman, D., 30, 31
Bond, R., 5, 41, 81, 83, 84, 85, 86, 88, 92
Bourdieu, P., 7, 10
Bowie, K., xii
Brack, D., 43
Brand, J., 17, 19, 20, 21, 23, 32
Brass, P. R., 122
Breuilly, J., 41
British Social Attitudes Survey, 82, 83t
Britishness, 123, 132
and being English, 5
elite views, 125–6, 129, 130
and Scottishness *see* Scottish vs British identity
Brown, A., 3, 5, 18, 39, 83
Brown, Gordon, 123

Bruce, Robert the, 107, 108, 110, 111, 112, 116
Budge, I., 39–40, 42, 43, 47, 48, 49–50
Burns, Robert, 8, 74

Cairney, P., 16, 18, 34, 48, 53
Calhoun, C., 41
Calman Commission (2007), 122
Campaign for a Scottish Assembly (CSA), 33
Charteris-Black, J., 64–5, 69–70
Chilton, P., 103, 104
Church of Scotland, 23
citizenship *see* Scottish passport, entitlement to
civic nationalism, 72–3
and education system, 3, 72
inclusive and exclusive elements, 76
interplay with non-civic nationalism, 13, 76
and legal system, 3, 39, 72
and Protestant church, 3, 23
and Scottish Parliament, 71–2
civil institutions, 39
Clydesidism, 23, 24
Coakley, J., 41
Cohen, A. P., 81–2
community languages, 70, 78
Comparative Manifesto Project (CMP)
analysis and coding, 42–4, 61, 167–9
categories/domains, 42–6; Economy, 44; External Relations, 44; Fabric of Society, 44–5; Freedom and Democracy, 42, 45, 48; Political System, 42, 44; Social Groups, 44; Welfare and Quality of Life, 44, 49